Nine Lives Plus

The Author after her round-the-world flight

The Hon. Mrs Victor Bruce

NINE LIVES PLUS

Record-breaking
on Land, Sea, and
in the Air

an autobiographical account

PELHAM BOOKS
LONDON

First published in Great Britain by
Pelham Books Ltd
52 Bedford Square
London WC1B 3EF
1977

ISBN 0 7207 0974 1

Filmset in 11 on 13 Baskerville
by DP Media, Hitchin,
printed in Great Britain by
Hollen Street Press Ltd at Slough,
and bound by James Burn at Esher, Surrey

To Tony, my Son

Contents

List of Illustrations

Foreword

I was on the A30 travelling towards the Thruxton motor racing circuit near Andover. A bright, sharp, sunny day held out the pleasures of my job: I drive fast cars for a living, and on this day in 1974 I looked forward to the added interest of meeting a living legend. For those of us who have read the history of motor racing with the avid interest of an enthusiast, the name Victor Bruce conjures up stories of superhuman endeavours, and records by the score: runs at Brooklands and in France and impressive feats of speed and endurance on the sea and in the air. I was to meet the Hon. Mrs Victor Bruce, who with her husband had for forty years been names alongside those of Segrave, Campbell and Cobb, and coupled with such famous vehicles as Bentley, Napier and Frazer Nash. To a schoolboy, they would be heroes: to an enthusiast, they are characters full of history and personality.

On my way to Thruxton, I had been overtaken by one of the most beautiful cars in the world: a Rolls Royce Phantom III with a Hooper Sedanca body. What a glorious sight! That's classic motoring, I thought. At Thruxton, the same beautiful Rolls was parked in the paddock. That fitted: the Hon. Mrs Victor Bruce could travel only in that style.

As Damon Runyon might say, when you meet Mrs Victor Bruce you are met. Immediately you shake hands, the personality is evident: quick conversation, bright alert eyes and a smiling disposition. She is ever ready with a word of comment, or ready to join in the conversation.

Britain has a tradition of record-breakers. On land, sea, and in the air, a Briton has at some time held a world record in every shape and form of car, boat and plane. The British motor industry created a great interest in motor racing, which spurred Cobb, Campbell and Segrave in their tremendous efforts. The husband-and-wife partnership of the Bruces contributed in no small way to this tradition. Endurance records at Brooklands and Montlhéry, arduous round-Europe and cross-Asia distance records, and high placings in the Monte Carlo Rally were all successes they earned. Unashamedly proud of her patriotic efforts, delighting in the glory her achievements brought to her country, the Hon. Mrs Victor Bruce exemplifies all that is good in our sporting heritage.

If one hesitates to ask why she attempted so many of these clearly dangerous feats because one fears the evasive 'because they were there' answer, one may gain an indication of the personal and patriotic satisfaction she gained from these record attempts by looking at the first England-France-England crossing of the Channel in an outboard. Reading her narrative, you feel that had the boat broken down, she would have been in the water in a trice, kicking for all she was worth, and pushing the boat before her. Let me assure you, knowing her, that this might well have happened.

People were incredulous at the time of her London to Japan flight, just eight weeks after her first flight; it is hard to imagine even today that anyone would have the sheer determination to scythe through all the negative attitudes and official discouragements like those she met. That Mrs Bruce had such determination is evident. To live life to the full has been her doctrine. Dedication, effort and luck have all played a part. Mrs Bruce would admit to having run risks, but she shows not the slightest devil-may-care attitude. She possesses the skills of planning, management and organisation: she is a figure to be respected. Her natural elegance and easy manner hide a strong and resolute character.

It is an uncanny experience to know a legend. One feels that the past is the present and the present the future. In her world of record-breaking, Mrs Bruce is a legend.

Stuart McCrudden
formerly Head of Motor Sport Operations
for the Ford Company in Europe

Introduction

THE LAST time I drove on a racetrack was at Thruxton near Andover in Hampshire on a lovely sunny day at the end of April 1974. I was 78½ years of age at the time and touched 110 m.p.h. down the straight, faster than I had ever driven in a long life that scarcely could have been called leisurely at any time.

Speed, in fact has always fascinated me since my first pony bolted. Going slowly always made me tired.

My Thruxton appearance was called splendidly the First Public Trial of the new three-litre Ford Ghia Capri. I was very flattered that those charming Ford executives should have asked someone of my age to put the pride of their designers and workshops through its paces.

It happened more or less by mistake. Three weeks previously I had been invited to go to Silverstone to see how the young men of today were getting on with racing cars which bore little resemblance to those I drove in the twenties and thirties.

Had I sat sedately in the stands, of course, I would have kept myself out of trouble; but once I saw those cars in action I simply had to have a closer look. So off I went in the general direction of the pits and that was where I met those nice Ford executives.

It seems that they had heard something about my Brooklands days for the next thing I knew they were introducing me to one of their works team, Peter Wardle, who was to drive an STP Surtees Allard in the John Player Atlantic race. He was about half a century younger than I was, but I soon found we had quite a lot in common – particularly Montlhéry race track outside Paris. In the twenties I had broken quite a few speed and endurance records there. The first time, my husband Victor and I had driven an AC car for ten days and ten nights, covering a distance of 15,000 miles.

Peter Wardle had driven there, too, a couple of score years later, of course. Together we talked each other round it almost yard by yard. It took me right back, I can tell you, and I soon gathered that the old place had not really changed very much. I remember Peter saying to me, 'There's a huge bump high up on the banking at one point.' I knew all about the bump, and I told him how Victor during the 15,000 mile record turned over on the ice-bound track because of that bump and wheel spin, and how he was buried under the car and escaped unhurt.

On a 24-hour record in a Bentley I hit that same bump every fifty-seven seconds, as I lapped the track. As a result it was almost a week before I could walk comfortably again.

For quite a while we exchanged our Montlhéry bump experiences; but as we talked my eyes kept straying to his Formula Atlantic car. It looked such a thoroughbred. Peter noticed my interest, and to my surprise and delight he asked me whether I would like to try it for size, which really was a compliment, because no driver likes strangers climbing in and out of his machine just before a race. In I climbed and took hold of the little steering-wheel, so different from the large ones I had known long ago. As I climbed out of the car again I said to Peter, 'I really must have another go on a track some day.'

One of the Ford executives heard me say this and asked me if I would like to test their new Ghia Capri on Thruxton track.

The thought of driving on a track again was pure joy for me, and of course I agreed.

Mind you I did not underestimate the task that faced me. I had not driven on a race track for something like forty years, not since I had been a member of the Alvis works team with John Cobb, who later broke the world land speed record. I had raced against men like Sir Henry Segrave, Sir Malcolm Campbell and Captain Frazer-Nash. My memory was good but motor cars had changed since those days: huge tyres now and tiny bodies, although the techniques of driving are much the same.

I decided that I had better put in a little practice before I appeared in public. Back home in Bradford-on-Avon a few days later I took my beautiful 1937 Phantom III Rolls Royce and put the pair of us through our paces along the roads of Wiltshire. I practised changing down through the gears and double-de-clutched as I used in the old days. Although for

1 The 1937 Rolls Royce Phantom III

many years I have driven cars with automatic gear boxes, I had not forgotten the old technique of changing down at high speed. I felt sure I should need to do this at Thruxton, as I had heard the finishing straight is very short and braking without the help of the gear box would not pull the car up at high speed.

On the day of the test I drove the Rolls to Thruxton. There I got my first surprise of the day. I had expected to find a few Ford and track officials waiting for me. Instead, as I drew to a stop outside the club house, I was surrounded by a swarm of motoring correspondents, cameramen, and television crews. The owner of the track, Mr Geoffrey Woodhouse, had flown over specially for the occasion in his private plane. Only then did I realise that it made news when someone of my generation set out to test a very fast car on what they told me was a very tricky track.

The journalists wanted to know, reasonably enough, how fast I was going to go, and whether I would try to beat the Thruxton lap record which John Surtees had set at an average of 120 m.p.h. I explained that the lap record was with a racing car and the Capri was a standard saloon car. I added that I would probably drive as fast as the car would go, but that I would decide when I saw the track.

Then I was introduced to Mr Stuart McCrudden who drives for the Ford company in rallies. He said to me, 'I'll drive the first circuit with you in the passenger seat to give you an idea of the corners and where you will need to brake and change down. Then you can take over, but this track is very tricky and it can take a professional driver a week or so to get used to it.'

I got into the passenger seat and off we drove. Soon we were doing about eighty and he was warning me of the awkward bits. When we came to what they call the Segrave corner he said, 'You've got to cling to the inner edge of the track. Keep clinging because this corner goes right round in almost a circle and at high speed when you reach the end of the corner the car will try to pull off the track, and you could end upside down in the rough.' Stuart reached this corner at about eighty miles per hour but he kept the car clinging to the edge. You could feel the pull of the car as we reached the end of the corner. Then down the finishing straight towards the grandstand. 'Not enough track', I thought to myself, 'at this speed.' Halfway to the stand Stuart said, 'Here you must brake, and if you think you can change down at high speed it will help.'

We pulled up at the club house and it was now my turn to drive. I was wearing the same little straw hat I had worn at Silverstone. Stuart explained that under the rules of the track I must wear a crash helmet and he produced one. I told him I never used such contraptions in my day and I put it on back to front. Stuart soon helped me to turn it round, and then we were off.

I was going pretty fast when I reached the first corner and I

2 Crash helmet on, and ready to go
Photo by courtesy of the London Express

clung closely to the edge, but as I neared the end of the corner the car tried to take charge. I quickly changed down at about seventy into third gear and managed to right the car and avoid the rough where so many drivers end up. Then one more corner and the finishing straight. I had no wish to break the Capri but did want to get the maximum speed out of her. So I asked Stuart to call out my speed after I had reached ninety as I wished to concentrate totally on driving the car.

I heard him say, 'Ninety . . . ninety-five . . . a hundred . . . hundred and five . . . hundred and ten . . . better brake now.' I did, but the grandstand was coming at me a little too quickly. I saw the escape road ahead and thought how humiliating it would be for me to go down that. In my day we despised racing drivers who had to use an escape road. It meant they were bad drivers. I changed quickly down into third gear, which helped, but not enough; so down into second and low gear. All was well; though I took the last bend with squealing tyres I pulled up in one piece in front of the club house.

I said to Stuart, 'You are brave to go round this track with a vintage driver like me. Were you afraid?'

'No,' he said. I told him I had been and he laughed. Actually I think he quite enjoyed it.

I soon learned, however, that the day was by no means over. I was asked endless questions: 'Was I frightened?'

'Only of the television cameras,' I said.

I had that day set a new personal speed record of 110 m.p.h., not difficult on a racing car but very tricky on a standard saloon. One or two of the track officials were admiring my Rolls. So I invited them to have a spin round the racetrack. I managed to squeeze in five – three journalists and two track officials. This wonderful car managed to top ninety on the track and they all enjoyed the experience.

This over, glasses appeared magically, and there was a whole series of toasts; to the Ghia Capri, to the Rolls, to Thruxton, to me, and to a lovely day. I had not enjoyed myself so much for a long time, although I took only a sip of champagne because I had to drive the Phantom home.

After that we went to the club house where I found another surprise waiting for me. I was introduced to Mr Geoffrey Heaton, who had volunteered to act as unpaid barman for the day. We had met before a little while back – forty-four years earlier, to be precise. He had been a very junior aircraft mechanic then; he had helped to service the *Bluebird*, the little aeroplane in which I had flown alone round the world in 1930. Together we talked of another age and another dimension, the air. That day my past certainly was catching up with me. There seemed to be an exciting memory around every corner.

After a buffet lunch it was time for me to say goodbye to my hosts who had been so kind to me. Stuart McCrudden walked me to my car, the pair of us still talking racing shop. Then I drove sedately home to Bradford-on-Avon.

The story of my test run, it seems, appeared in newspapers and on television all over the world. Letters began to flow in from the most unlikely spots. Some from old friends, and some from people I had never met. There was one letter from a lady who lived in the Soviet Union. Another came from a lady in Australia. She wrote to say that she had just reached her fortieth birthday and had been feeling that life was virtually over. Then she had read about me circling Thruxton at the age of 78½. She went on, 'That made me take a completely new view of the future. You made me realise that I had many, many useful years ahead of me, that life was only beginning. And I'm going to live it.'

Until that letter I had looked on my Thruxton experience as a splendid day out with a fast car in pleasant company. That stranger in Australia, however, made me feel that perhaps I had accomplished something useful. Unknowingly I had given new hope and strength to someone on the other side of the world, and maybe to others too.

For many months afterwards I continued to get letters about Thruxton. Some wrote to ask me how I got involved with motor racing and flying: that's not an easy question to answer – perhaps the answer lies in history.

Both sides of my family, one American, the other English speckled with Irish, lived and fought and died adventurously, and generally with some style.

I think, perhaps, that their spirits have fused in me and caused the chain reaction of explosions which this book is about.

One
Early Days

ABOUT once a week my mother used to throw her hands high and say to me in tones of doom: 'You've nine lives, like a cat!' I think she underestimated, because I must be working through my tenth or eleventh by now.

I could never understand why she was so surprised that I emerged more or less unscathed and unscarred from car, plane and even horse crashes, to say nothing of a near miss with a liner when I was trying to beat a speed boat record. After all, there is a heavy history of survival on both sides of the family, stretching back over the centuries. We all seemed to have shared this extremely useful feline asset of having a few lives to spare.

My great grandmother had it. She was born in Kentucky. In 1849 she trekked across the plains in the famous gold rush to California. There were 122 at the start of that epic journey and 21 when they reached their destination. My great-grandmother was one of them. Not only was she the life and soul of the party in face of constant danger, but she ended up their leader.

She used to tell my mother that the gold in California was so near the surface that they just had to pull up the grass to collect it. She was exaggerating a little there, of course, but she was not exaggerating when she described the birth of my grandmother.

The party was being attacked by Indians. She was lying under the covered waggon, firing through the spokes of the wheel, when she broke off to have her baby which, like herself, survived the trip in spite of numerous other attacks.

On the English side of the family there was Sir William Petre. I'd say he had more lives than I've had. He was Tudor Secretary to four monarchs: Henry VIII; Edward VI, the weakling who died very soon after becoming King; Bloody Mary, a Catholic; and Queen Elizabeth, a Protestant. He survived them all. He kept his head metaphorically and physically at a time when many others were losing theirs in both senses.

One of his more unpleasant jobs was taking the keys away from the monasteries and convents during the reign of Henry VIII. His last call, coincidentally, was at Malmesbury, the abbey near where I live now in Bradford-on-Avon in Wiltshire. History, I'm glad to say, records that he carried out this task with tact and sympathy. When he took the keys there was never any unpleasantness, such as ravishing or looting. Both these extravagances were inclined to happen when others took the keys.

He was, indeed, a man of sensitivity. Whenever there was a burning at the stake, he was expected to attend. He always made the excuse that he had a sore throat and retired to his home in Ingatestone Hall; he would explain that he had to look after the plumbing.

Another of my ancestors was the third Earl of Derwentwater, a first cousin of King James III. He was not quite so fortunate as Sir William Petre, but he gave his enemies quite a run for their money and his own honour.

He fought for his cousin, King James III, in his struggle for the throne. Both had to leave England. He returned again to raise an army, but this time was captured and sent to the Tower. He was sentenced to death and there was no escape, but at least he lost his last life with style.

In those days execution etiquette required the condemned man to tip the gaoler who escorted him to the scaffold. The Earl of Derwentwater was still joking on that last walk. When he reached the scaffold he turned to the gaoler and said with a smile, 'You know, this is all the wrong way round. You should be tipping me!'

Then he examined the block carefully and said, 'That's too rough for my neck. Get someone to smooth it out.' They did so. Coolly he put his neck on the block and said, 'Strike when I say "Jesus" three times.' They respected that last wish. In fact he seemed to be giving all the orders at his own execution.

His wife had kept writing to him when he was in the Tower, saying, 'Stand firm. Don't give way!' They really were made of fine material in those days. He held to his faith and accepted his fate without argument. I don't think I'd have been quite like that. I'd have argued all the way to the scaffold. I'd have had plenty to say about it.

My mother and in his early days my father were scarcely orthodox either, come to think of it. Mama's brothers were actor-managers in America and they soon saw her potential as an actress. She began her career with Shakespeare, playing Juliet at the age of seventeen. She was an immediate success, and her brothers arranged for her to come to London, where she played at the Gaiety Theatre.

She was thoroughly versatile, able to play in the greatest tragedies one night and switch the following night to musical comedy. Shakespeare, however, remained her great love. When there were parties in our house she would recite for the guests, and I used to sneak downstairs to listen outside the door. I always remember her chilling my spine with the curse of Queen Anne on Richard III: 'Hung be the heavens in black . . .' A few minutes later she would sit at the piano and start playing light-hearted airs brilliantly; or she would pick up a ukelele and give a performance which would not have shamed George Formby.

Success came to her quickly, but her career was short. While she was appearing at the Gaiety, the producer of *The Belle of New York* saw her and decided immediately that she was the star, the Belle, the Salvation Army lassie he wanted for the show which had yet to have its première. He offered her £100 a week (a fortune in those days), and she accepted.

She never played the rôle, however, because there was somebody else in the audience who wanted to sign her up for a different role – my father. Night after night he had sat in the stalls, clapping like mad. He began courting her with determination – so persistently, in fact, that they became engaged a few months later. *The Belle of New York* won immediate fame with a different Salvation Army lassie in the star rôle. Mama turned her back on Broadway, married Dada and moved to his home, Coptfold Hall in Essex. It was a very large house, a lonely, distant place that was a world away from the bright lights of New York. She had to pass through a mile of woodland to reach it, and I think there were many times when she sighed over her decision. When I was about six she dressed all my dolls as Salvation Army lassies in a mood of what-might-have-been.

My parents were in fact an ill-suited couple. Mama used to say to me, 'Your father is a gloomy man – lugubrious.' At that time I wasn't quite sure what lugubrious meant, but I remember asking her, 'If he's gloomy, why did you marry him?' Quietly, but firmly she replied, 'I married him to keep him quiet, to shut him up.'

Yet in his early days he can't have been so lugubrious. Before he married, he lived for some time at Thorndon Hall, Brentwood – until part of it was burned down, the largest house in Britain. His fellow residents were his uncle (the thirteenth Lord Petre, a priest who was a Monsignor of the Vatican), a vast staff, and fifteen pointer dogs. When he married, incidentally, Dada took not only his bride to Coptfold Hall, but the fifteen pointers, too. Mama said every single one had fleas.

Despite his uncle's lofty position in the Church, my father was scarcely priestly material. Even Lloyds of London were prepared to bet on that; and they did so in rather complicated circumstances which I can explain only by delving a little further back into the family history.

My grandmother, a daughter of the Earl of Wicklow, married the Hon. Arthur Petre, into a family which had always been Catholic. The Earl of Wicklow, a staunch and, if I may say so rather bigotted Protestant, left a large fortune, and stated in his will that not a penny would go to any member of the family who became a priest or a nun. Furthermore he tied it up (entailed it, the lawyers say), to the third generation. That meant that whoever inherited it could have only the interest on the capital.

At that time (throughout his life, for that matter) my father was short of money. I think he spent a good deal of time in London, presumably leaving his uncle the Monsignor alone in the mighty acres of Thorndon Hall to exercise the pointers. Anyway, Dada decided that he would try to borrow some money on his life interest on the capital which the Earl of Wicklow had tied up so successfully. The family lawyers, however, pointed out that he couldn't do so, because later on in life he might become a priest.

Now that was one obstacle which had never crossed Dada's mind. So off he went to Lloyds and said that he wanted to insure against this terrible risk that he might take Holy Orders. They took one look at him in his very fashionable Savile Row suit with a fresh red carnation in the button hole, and agreed without hesitation to issue a policy for no more than a nominal fee.

Shortage of money throughout his life was one reason why he was gloomy. It was the gloom, rather than the financial difficulties, which caused the main rift between Mama and himself, however. Nevertheless, they had four sons fairly rapidly. Then I was born, an event which caused quite a furore of excitement in a house which had no daughter. Mama told me later that my father smiled for the first time in years when my arrival was announced. Later they had another son; but sadly three of my little brothers died when they were babies, leaving only my brother Louis, myself, and later Roderick.

My own first memories go back to the time when I was two years old; I remember playing ball with one of my brothers under the nursery table. I also remember becoming absolutely furious with a donkey we owned called Paddy. I used to ride him sitting securely in a basket chair, while my nurse hovered close, ready for any emergency landing. But even then I yearned for speed. I couldn't get Paddy to go fast enough. We must have been a strange sight, indeed – frantic nurse, ambling donkey and two-year-old girl, the last bouncing in a basket chair with frustration.

From the time I was two until I was six must have been the most uneventful years of my life because I can't remember

3 Myself aged two, peering over the parapet of the pony trap, with my governess and brother Louis

them at all. When I was six, however, my mother insisted that my father should buy me a very small Shetland pony, called Dinky. I shall never forget Dinky. He was frisky and used to bolt. Everyone used to have hysterics on those occasions: I was hysterical with delight.

When I was nine my mother decided I should have something bigger. So off we went together to the dealer. I remember Mama asking him whether this particular pony was quiet to ride and drive. The dealer said, 'Absolutely.' Immediately I began nudging my mother and whispering, 'Please don't buy him, Mama. I don't want him. I want something that runs away.'

The dealer heard me and said that the pony might liven up a bit if it had some corn; but I was adamant. Mama got me instead a really lively Welsh pony which suited me perfectly. It used to bolt, too. Over the next few years it wrecked two governess carts by hurling them – and me – into ditches. After the pair of us had broken the second governess cart the insurance company refused to cover me any more.

My mother, who was highly emotional, used to create splendidly dramatic scenes about all these escapades. She used to make me promise solemnly that I would never ever take risks again; but I think deep down she enjoyed it all thoroughly. She was a wonderful woman who thrived on adventure, even if it was only a governess cart crashing into a ditch.

My father took a different view. Whenever one of my ponies ran away he would insist that it must be sold, which of course led to tearful scenes. He kept worrying about the cost of buying new governess carts, which was understandable, because, as I have said, he always had financial problems. When he inherited Coptfold Hall he became Lord of the Manor and was responsible for the entire estate. It needed a staff of at least fifteen to run and he had to find the money to pay them.

Unfortunately my grandmother Lady Catherine Howard was obsessed with writing codicils to her will in much the same way that I was obsessed with speed. She kept putting people into her will and taking others out, as if she were playing some crazy game of musical legacies. She managed to write twelve codicils, which must be something of a record. The family solicitors got into such a muddle with them that my father ended up inheriting the estate without any money to run it properly. If it had not been for all these codicils he would have inherited a large fortune. Eventually the dispute ended up in a law suit over the will. For two years everything seemed to hang on this case. While it was pending, I was constantly told that I would get a new pony or a new governess cart or a new this or a new that 'as soon as Dada wins his case'.

But Dada lost his case, and that was the gloomiest day of all, because he *should* have had his share. The economies became harsher than ever, although my mother fought them every inch of the way. When my father heard that she was buying me a cob to replace the Welsh pony he said, 'You're getting those ponies bigger and bigger. They're eating more and more.' Mama said haughtily, 'If she wants a new pony, she'll have a new pony.' And Mama won as usual. I was completely spoiled – and a born show-off into the bargain.

It was when the case was finally lost that my Aunt Maud made a gesture, and left me a very small legacy which I was later to put to good use. I squeezed it out of the family solicitor, and used the money to launch myself into the world of professional motor racing.

I always managed to emerge from the governess cart crashes with no more than minor cuts and bruises, probably due to the fact that my one surviving brother, Louis (five years my senior), was putting me through quite a toughening-up course.

It was for his benefit, of course, not for mine. He was a fanatical cricketer, a fast bowler. When I was nine he used to pay me a penny an hour if I'd let him bowl at me with a hard cricket ball instead of a soft tennis ball. So long as he paid up, I played up. I never let him know that I enjoyed it, because that news might have cut off my source of extra income.

He was also a keen fencer. So I had to fence with him. For some reason or other these contests always took place on a little roof garden we had on top of a shed: there he would be, lunging at me, while I had my back to a drop of five feet.

That was when we were living in London. We always had a house in town and a second house in the country, another reason, I suppose, why my father never had much spare money. Because Mama, like myself, liked moving about, we were always changing the second house. I remember living at Herne Bay, at Taplow near Maidenhead, and at Osterley Park. Altogether there were seven changes, which meant that I went to seven different convent schools, introducing, if I remember rightly, riot conditions into each. I was not a scholar, being particularly bad at arithmetic. I still can't do sums. This disability, however, has neither bothered nor hindered me throughout my life. Once, when my mother asked me what I wanted to be when I grew up, I said, 'A millionaire.' I was serious, and she took me seriously: she didn't laugh, but replied simply, 'I think that's a very good idea.'

I was to achieve my ambition by making a million dollars.

In all my schools I won only one prize. For some extraordinary reason which I could not understand then, and cannot now, it was for piety. I can only conclude that it was a consolation prize. It was just about this time that I made my first small piece of motoring history. I became the first girl in Britain to ride a motor cycle on the open road – and the first girl to appear in court on a motoring charge.

Indirectly it was my brother's fault. At what must have been one of the first Motor Shows, he had bought for £120 a Matchless motor-cycle and sidecar, a beautiful, shining piece of machinery with an eight-horsepower engine. He paid for it himself, as he too had been left a small legacy, and he bought his own petrol. Dada was delighted, saying that it was much more economical than a pony because it didn't eat anything.

I was delighted too, by the very sight of it. I remember gazing at it in wonder and saying to myself, 'Just imagine . . . eight runaway ponies!' Naturally I asked Louis if I could ride it, but he replied rather loftily, 'Don't be childish! You're a girl'.

Soon afterwards, however, he went to Germany for a few months. Before he left he asked me to look after his motor-bike, by polishing it. I fear I interpreted his instructions a little too liberally. I felt that he would like me to exercise it for him too.

We were living in Osterley Park at the time. As soon as Louis left I got a young chap who worked in the village's new garage to come round and show me what made a motor-cycle tick. He said, 'It's easy. There's nothing to it', gave me lessons for half an hour on the tennis court, and after that I was on my own.

Round and round the tennis court I rode with my collie dog Laddie in the sidecar. With each circuit I gained confidence, until I was certain I had those eight ponies under complete control. Then my mother arrived back from the village in her gig and created her usual fine drama with her usual superb professionalism.

'Don't you dare ride that thing', she said in tones of vibrant doom. 'You'll kill yourself. I know it!'

Luckily for me, she was not only an adventurous person, but volatile too. She could change her mind with the wind. I said, 'But it's so easy, Mama. Here . . . you sit in the sidecar and I'll show you.'

She hesitated for only a moment. I lifted Laddie out, and my mother climbed into the sidecar. I drove her once round the

4 Britain's first motor-cyclist? Myself aged 15¾ on Louis's Matchless motor-cycle

tennis court and then out onto the road. By the time we reached home again she had been converted totally to the virtue of motor-cycles and seemed to have forgotten completely her absolute conviction of half an hour earlier that I was going to kill myself on one.

From that day on I was scarcely out of the saddle of Louis's bike. I wore my hair in plaits then, tied with big red bows. I put another red bow on my team-mate, Laddie, and together we rode up and down the highways and byways of Hounslow, throwing up clouds of dust in our wake. To my delight I found that I could push my speed up to between fifty-five and sixty miles an hour, which in 1911 was rather like breaking the sound barrier today. To lighten the bike and get a few extra miles an hour out of it, I then took the baffles out of the silencer.

I don't know whether or not this ploy succeeded, but to me the roar of the engine was exhilarating, and it certainly made me feel as if I was going faster. Unfortunately other residents in the neighbourhood were not quite so exhilarated. One day I emerged from a cloud of dust to find a policeman standing in the middle of the road, his hand held high. PC Parker, six feet and one inch tall, very good looking, and very smart, was seemingly very angry.

'May I ask what you are doing with this machine?'

It was a good question. I knew I would have to think and talk fast if I was going to scramble out of trouble. Doing my best to look sorry I said, 'I'm . . . practising.'

The answer did not seem to impress him. He didn't even bother to ask me what or why I was practising. He said only, 'Do you realise that local residents have been complaining about the noise you're making? That engine sounds like a bomb exploding, and furthermore you've been going much too fast.'

I hung my head and tried to look contrite. Laddie gazed at him plaintively, as if he sensed that his motor-cycling days were drawing to a close. PC Parker was quite unmoved by our joint performance. He took my name and address and said ominously, 'You'll be hearing more about this, young lady.'

The next day he called at my home and handed me a summons. Luckily my mother was out, and nobody else saw him, which meant that I could keep this dark and terrible secret to myself for a while at least. When he left I looked at the piece of frightfully official-looking paper and saw that I had been summonsed for causing a public nuisance on the highway and for speeding. I had to appear in court two days later.

I rode to court on the motor-cycle, Laddie beside me. He sat quietly in the sidecar while I went in to stand my trial before the magistrate in Hounslow police court. When I was marched into the dock his eyebrows lifted a fraction of an inch, because I bore little resemblance to his usual customers.

PC Parker, his face utterly expressionless, gave evidence about the complaints, the noise, the speed. He told the court of our encounter in the lane near Osterley Park, and gave a thoroughly accurate word-for-word account of our brief conversation. Then he stood down. The magistrate and I gazed at each other for a while, the pair of us, I think, bewildered by a situation to which we were unaccustomed. At last he said, 'How old are you, young lady?'

In almost a whisper I replied, 'Fifteen and three-quarters, Sir . . . nearly.' Again there was silence for a moment, as if I had presented him with some obscure point in law. Then, 'Have you a licence for this contraption?'

Now at the time the licensing system differed from that of today. You paid a pound a wheel for a horse-drawn vehicle. A governess cart, which had two wheels, cost £2; a brougham with four wheels, £4. In desperation I tried to suggest that the motor-cycle had three wheels and therefore fell between these two legal stools. For good measure I added, 'I've a licence for my dog, Sir. He's waiting for me outside.'

Looking back across some sixty-five years I can see that my defence was inclined to be on the weak side. It was, however, the best I could manage on the spur of the moment, and incredibly it seemed to carry some weight. In a tired, almost resigned voice, the magistrate pronounced, 'I am banning you from riding that motor-bicycle for one year. You will pay six shillings costs.'

Luckily I had the money with me. I used to get half-a-crown per week pocket money from my father, and saved most of it for petrol. All the same, I left that court heart-broken, divorced from the joy of my life for twelve long months. The garage lad who had taught me to ride the bike rode it home for me, while Laddie and I followed slowly and sadly on foot.

That was not by any means the end of my problems. I had to tell my mother and, worse still my father, that their daughter had been charged in the local police court, bringing shame and disgrace on the family. That night I went to my mother's bedroom and stood silently for a moment as she combed her beautiful hair at the dressing table. Then I said, 'Mama . . . I've something terrible to tell you.'

The brush froze in mid-air. She said nothing, but I could see the reflection of her eyes, wide and fearful, staring at me from the mirror. I stammered, 'I . . . I've been in the police court.'

The storm broke quickly and as usual, dramatically.

'Heavens!' she said, 'This is the end! What will we do? What are we coming to now?'

I waited for her to continue, quite sure that I had heard only the overture. To my amazement she said no more. I waited for her to faint. She wasn't even swaying, just sitting there motionless. I was so relieved that I said almost brightly, 'Don't worry, Mama. I haven't burgled or anything. It's about the bike and speeding and making a noise and he hasn't even fined me. He let me off with six shillings costs and said I wasn't to ride the bike for another year.'

My mother, who a moment earlier must have thought I had injured someone, was quite calm and logical now. With a sigh she said, 'Perhaps that's a mercy. Now how are we going to break the news to your father?'

It was a rhetorical question, for she had decided already that she would tell him herself. She kept quiet about the affair for a day, presumably choosing her moment with scrupulous care. Then she told him that his daughter had been in a little trouble with the law. When he heard the details he gave me a long lecture, but to the amazement of the pair of us, he did not have apoplexy. This stain on the family escutcheon, it seemed, was more than counterbalanced by the saving which could result from my twelve months ban. He was always a little suspicious about the motor-bike. He could never quite believe that it wasn't costing him any money. He always expected, I think, that one day it would dive into his pocket in one way or another. So when he had finished reading the riot act to me, he said, 'I'm pleased you can't ride that machine any more. It's much too big for you . . . and much too expensive to run.'

I had weathered two storms, but nevertheless I remained grounded; and when you're fifteen and three-quarters (nearly), a year seems a century. Yet that one passed, as years will, and at last to my huge joy I was able to take the motor-bike out again. By that time my brother had returned from Germany, bought himself a car and lost interest in the bike. So it was virtually mine.

I painted it red to match the ribbons which Laddie and I still wore and I went back to the road again, venturing further afield this time, perhaps partly because I wanted to get well away from PC Parker's bailiwick, but mainly because of the sheer joy I found in riding on and on and on. I rode to London, which at that time still belonged mainly to the horse. Crowds cheered as I went by. Even the policemen seemed glad to see me and shouted, 'Bravo!' Bus drivers slowed down for me, waved me on, and shouted, 'The road is yours!'

On another occasion I rode down to one of my old convents in Herne Bay to see my favourite nun, Madame Sacre Coeur, a young, slim, and attractive girl, full of fun and just out of the novice stage. She had never seen anything wrong in any of my escapades. She just thought I was acting like any high-spirited girl would.

She gazed in awe and admiration at the motor-bike. I knew what was in her mind and I put it into words. I said, 'Get on the pillion, Sister. I'll give you a spin round the tennis court.'

Her eyes gleamed. Then she said, 'Reverend Mother wouldn't let me.'

I knew the Reverend Mother was out and I told her so. She hesitated for only a moment. Then, hoisting her robes a trifle, she sat side-saddle on the pillion, her arms round my waist. I drove gently round the tennis court and that was how Madame Sacre Coeur made motoring history by being the first nun to travel on a motor-bike.

Eventually and inevitably, perhaps, I myself created another little slice of history by being the first girl to crash a motor-cycle. I had ridden to Brighton with a friend in the sidecar. As we moved reasonably slowly down the promenade I saw a beautiful car parked outside the Metropole Hotel. I reacted to that car as another girl might to the sight of a Paris gown in a Bond Street shop. I just gazed at the car in wonder, hypnotized by its beauty. While I was in this trance, the wheel of the sidecar touched a passing taxi, and over went the motor-bike.

We weren't hurt, just a bit shaken. The consternation we caused, however, was quite spectacular. It was as if a couple of astronauts had landed on the prom today. Holiday-makers gathered round, got the motor-bike right way up and treated us like a couple of heroines. The back tyre had been knocked off, but in no time they had it on again. We went away amid cheers from the crowd.

The 1914 – 18 war put the end to my joy-riding. My father sold the motor-cycle, because he felt that we should all tighten our belts and that the sight of a young girl roaring round the country on an expensive machine when times were hard was a bad example. Before that tragic event, however, I very nearly made a contribution to the war effort that would have done little to help the Allied cause. In 1914 I was riding down Whitehall, when I nearly obliterated several members of His Majesty's General Headquarters Staff who were crossing the road opposite the War Office. They were very nice about it. Like good soldiers they jumped back smartly and applauded as I swept by.

I was sad to lose the bike, of course, but I appreciated the point my father was making. So instead of fretting I began making plans for peacetime. I decided I wanted a car – a fast car with a leather strap around the bonnet, like those they used on the race tracks. From that moment on I began saving hard.

By the time the war ended, I was a good distance from my financial target. By 1920 I had £75, half the price of an Enfield Allday, a well-known make in those days, which could touch 75 m.p.h.; and it was then that my parents, who had been watching my efforts quietly, stepped in to help. My mother gave me a quarter of the price and my father the other quarter. My dream had come true, and I hoped that some day I would become a racing motorist.

But times had changed. The policemen were not shouting 'bravo' any more. The bus drivers were not telling me the road was mine. The sight of a woman behind the wheel of a car or on a motor-cycle was no longer a novelty. They had driven ambulances in France, and done men's work in factories. It was a new era.

Cars were no longer novelties, either. Motorists had ceased to be dare-devil gladiators, racing towards an exciting future.

As they increased in numbers, public opinion changed, and they were seen as murderous menaces, operating noisy, smelly, dangerous machines. Instead of cheering me, pedestrians shook their fists.

Most of the police seemed to side with the pedestrians: some took positive pleasure in summonsing motorists. We were living in Kensington then, and from time to time I used to race down to Brighton in my car. But one day I was stopped by a policeman in the Bayswater Road. Almost triumphantly he said, 'We've been trying to trap you for weeks, Miss, but you've been a bit too fast for us until now.'

'Trap me?' I said. 'What do you mean by that?' He smiled, and for the first time I noticed a stop watch in his hand. Then up panted one of his colleagues, and suddenly I realised what I was up against. One of them had been hiding behind a tree or in the shadow of a building further down the road. As I'd buzzed by, he had jumped out to signal his friend, who immediately started his stop watch.

They then measured the distance between them carefully. In that way they could judge my speed. It may sound a rough and ready method in these days of radar traps, but believe me it worked – or at least it was accepted by the magistrates. Certainly that occasion led to what was my first, but by no means last, appearance in Bow Street police court.

Most times I managed to beat the police traps by sheer speed, passing the second policeman before he had time to start his watch. I couldn't win them all, however, and one week I appeared before the Bow Street magistrate three days running; by the third day he was getting a little tired of me. Fining me ten shillings, quite a lot of money in those days, he snapped, 'Young lady, you're making a career in my court.'

I had, I suppose, broken a record, one which probably still stands. Even today I doubt if there are many motorists around who have appeared in court on separate speeding charges three days running. Looking back, I realise that it is not a record in which I can take pride: I knew then that as soon as I took up competitive driving I would have to be sensible.

Two

The Monte Carlo Rally 1927

SEVERAL years were to pass before my geat chance came, when I was able to enter a car for the Monte Carlo Rally. I was then living near the AC car factory at Thames Ditton. The managing director, I expect, became tired of my repeated requests to borrow a car to enter for this trial. After refusing many times, he suddenly said, 'Yes.' S.F. Edge was his name, and a great sportsman he was. In 1907 he created a twenty-four hour single-handed record, driving around Brooklands day and night: he practically wore the track out, he told me, and great pieces had come away as he drove.

The rules for the Monte Carlo Rally in the late twenties allowed competitors to select their own starting points: one man chose Tunis, in Africa, a thousand miles further than anyone else. He would surely have won if he hadn't driven into a river and ruined his engine. Marks were given for distance, average speed, and the number of passengers carried. This last was not a good idea, since one passenger was equivalent to five hundred miles. The year I entered first, a man had started from Stockholm in a motor bus, with twenty passengers. This was a farce. Had the bus not slid into a ditch and been too heavy to pull out, he might well have won.

I decided to start from John O'Groats; my passengers were three: Bobby Beare, motoring editor of the *Daily Sketch*, the engineer, and my husband Victor.

I had met Victor at the AC factory: he was a member of the AC works team, and raced for Mr Edge. He had won the 1926 Monte Carlo Rally, being the first Englishman to do so.

From John O'Groats to Monte Carlo is seventeen hundred miles. I went down with flu and a temperature of 103° the night before we left. But we started regardless, and the germs must have found the pace too hot, for by the time we reached Perth I seemed to be fit again. Scotland was entirely under snow, and it was very difficult keeping to the road over the Grampian mountains, since it was almost impossible to see it in places. We had decided not to stop for food until we reached Blair Atholl, as we were anxious to be done with the mountains before nightfall.

5 The start from the John O'Groats Hotel

Our first official control was at the Headquarters of the Royal Scottish Automobile Club, Glasgow, where we stopped for a bowl of soup. But with the first spoonful, the promised weather report arrived in a telegram: 'Thick fog fifty miles round Carlisle, mist on Yorkshire Moors, heavy snow falling from London onwards, frozen roads very dangerous.' Interest in the soup fled and we left the table. We had not travelled far before we struck the expected fog, and for the next two or three hundred miles had to battle our way through, emerging from the fog only to enter a blizzard. Once again it became almost impossible to distinguish the line of the road. With a sigh of relief we reached Doncaster, the next control point.

By dawn I had been driving for sixteen hours. It had been announced, by some mistake in the press, that I intended to drive single-handed all the way to Monte Carlo. I felt sure I couldn't do this. Sleepiness was the next hazard, the dawn being the worst time. After 24 hours continuous driving, we reached the second control point at Leicester Square. A large crowd – many more than expected – had come out to welcome us and wish us well on our way. Whether it was the excitement or just that I was tired I don't know, but I suddenly felt very shaky. Someone gave me a drink which I thought was ginger ale: it may have been brandy. I suddenly felt all right again, and decided to continue at the wheel as far as Folkestone, and then call it a day.

On the outskirts of London we began to overtake some competitors from Doncaster who were in an open car. We were thankful that we had such a cosy saloon. I was still at the wheel when we reached Folkestone, having covered the distance from London in a surprisingly short time. There was just half an hour left before the boat sailed. I had hoped to have a rest crossing the Channel, but was too excited and couldn't sleep. Before realising what had happened I was back at the wheel again driving over the ice-bound roads to Paris. My passengers were a splendid help, because it is not particularly pleasant to be driven at high speed over frozen and fog-bound roads. Victor seemed quite happy acting as navigator, and Bobby Beare and G. Pitt the engineer took turns at gently tapping my head to keep me awake. We reached Paris at midnight where we checked at the third control. We were well ahead of time, and so managed to have a sandwich and some strong coffee. 'Only six hundred miles to go to reach Monte Carlo,' one of my passengers said. Only six hundred miles indeed; fifty miles seems a long way when you are dead tired. The news had already been given to the press that I was still at the wheel. In those days it was a novelty for a woman to drive such a long distance, and I began to think how I might turn the publicity for the AC to good account, especially if I could win the Ladies' Cup driving single-handed; so the third dawn found me crossing the Esterel Mountains, with frightful chasms yawning at every unprotected hairpin: I think there were literally hundreds in those days, all straightened out now by by-passes. It was only by driving very fast that I was able to keep awake, and

6 The roads to Paris were ice-bound

even so I kept thinking there were big black dogs crossing the road. The reward was to come, for as the dawn arrived we saw the blue waters of the Mediterranean. All of a sudden, I felt tired no more. The surface of the mountain road had been dreadful, full of potholes, but once we reached Cannes the road was smooth all the way to Monte Carlo. We clocked in outside the Casino dead on time, after I had been seventy hours and twenty minutes at the wheel since leaving John O'Groats.

7 Asleep at the wheel after seventy-two hours non-stop driving from John O'Groats to Monte Carlo

That was not the end of the Rally, however, because the following day the competitors had to take part in the Alpine test over the Col de Bras, with its many hairpin bends and frozen roads. This test is more or less a road race, and there are secret checks, and to have any hope of a place in the final marking you have to be dead on time to the split second. The going was certainly very tricky that next morning. High up on the mountain the little car slid all over the road, while all we could do was hope for the best. Suddenly we came round a bend to find that two cars had crashed into each other, and one was hanging nearly over the parapet. I dared not use the brakes on that ice, so I couldn't stop, and could only steer to avoid them. We squeezed through.

The next day, when the results were announced, I found I had won the Coupe des Dames. Victor had won the Rally the year before. We were all very happy that day.

8 I receive the Coupe des Dames, outside the Prince's palace at Monte Carlo

Mr Edge had suggested that if we reached Monte Carlo safely, we should then carry out an official distance trial over about eight thousand miles. He arranged with the Royal Automobile Club to send an observer to Monte Carlo to make notes regarding the performance of the AC. We chose as our route a journey down the leg of Italy, across the straits of Messina to Sicily and from there by ship to Tunis in Northern Africa. We were then to drive along the African coast to Tangier, cross the Straits and return through Spain to England.

We were looking forward to this tour, but felt a little anxious when we were told by an official of the Automobile Association that we would be very lucky if we succeeded in driving our car very far south of Naples. He explained that at that time of the year, some of the bridges would be down, and that the roads were so bad we would probably break the springing on the car.

Just the same I was still determined to take a chance. So on 28 January after an enthusiastic send-off from the members of the Sporting Club of Monaco we started our arduous journey. We took as an extra passenger Mr Johnson, motoring editor of *Country Life*. He came to take photographs of the many interesting places we were going to see. All went well as far as Genoa. Then the roads became so rough, with potholes two or three feet deep, that our average speed was only ten miles an hour as far as Rome. But I think we all thought that the misery of the

9 The rough roads of Italy

rough roads was worthwhile, because none of us had seen Pisa or Rome.

After Naples we did not enjoy the journey at all. The poverty in the towns we passed through depressed us, as did especially the cruelty to animals. We were cheered, however, when we met a man in southern Italy who was organising a society for the prevention of cruelty to animals.

We were not allowed to go far without excitement. After leaving Tiriolo we came across a huge rock which had fallen down the mountain side. There was just room for the car to squeeze through, but a few miles further on we came to more rocks and a notice in Italian. We looked at our Italian–English dictionary: 'Danger'. Blasting operations seemed most likely, but I drove on. Then round the next corner we found the cause of the stones which had indeed been placed there for a purpose. There was a broken bridge across a wide river: it looked as though this was going to end our journey. We found some labourers sitting beside the bridge. We tried to explain to them that we must get across the river, but all they kept saying was

10 A road on the outskirts of Naples

'Napoli', telling us to go back to Naples.

We knew there was one thing that they would understand – money. Even English pounds. We showed them about £10, and they started to run some planks across the broken centre of the bridge. When the planks had been fixed, the time had come for me to drive across the bridge. Of course it may have been coincidence, but two of my passengers developed a different excuse for remaining out of the car. One suggested it would lighten the load if he got out, and the other decided it was the right moment for him to take a ciné film. All went well until I

11 Crossing the broken bridge

was half way across, when the tool box jammed on a plank. Fortunately, the labourers developed a fit of energy, unusual in that part of the world, and lifted the car over the plank. They seemed as pleased as we were that we had got across.

Eventually we arrived at Villa San Giovanni, in good time for the last ferry boat of the day to Messina. A long drive the next day brought us to Palermo, the finest town we had visited since leaving Rome. We then drove to the quay just in time to catch the boat to Tunis where we had been warned to look out for pick-pockets. The first Arab we met was a very elaborate individual. We learned later that he was connected with a gang which posed as members of the shipping company. He was dressed in the latest thing in striped bath gowns – a 'burnous' I suppose the garment would be called. We soon found out that we were going to be 'had'. Ali Baba we called this man, who took away our Carnet and shipping papers, then demanded 700 francs. By now we were surrounded by his forty thieves, who obstructed our path to the customs control.

Rather than run the risk of losing our documents, we handed

12 In Moroccan towns,
there was always great interest shown in our AC

over the money. Except for this unfortunate experience, we enjoyed our journey along the coast of North Africa; the roads were good, and we found the other Arabs most helpful and very interested in our little car. On the way to Tangier we drove to Laghouat, right in the heart of the desert and a lonely place. We had to follow a track, and be very careful not to leave it, for if we did it might be days or even weeks before we were found. The only thing of interest we saw between the towns was a miniature army of humans and camels. It was a remarkable sight: whole families were piled up on the camels, complete with luggage, and a number of baby camels were trotting alongside. We were told that certain tribes march to the mountains at about that time of the year.

The next place of interest was Fez in French Morocco. The town is surrounded by a high wall. In the centre was a luxurious hotel, formerly the Sultan's palace. The harem had not been changed, and if one wished one could sit on the floor on comfortable cushions while your meals were served on little tables, thus keeping the atmosphere of the palace. The manager of the hotel led us into a beautiful garden then through a gateway into a secluded place – balconied and paved with mosaic. He told us we were now in the harem. We then followed him into the chamber of the Sultana.

I had never seen such a fantastic room. The walls were studded with semi-precious jewels, and the doors inlaid with pure gold. The manager, who was intrigued by our tour, said we could use the Sultana's chamber for the night. The garden

13 Outside the Sultana's bedroom

had a small pool with a fountain, and by moonlight it was enchanting. Above the chamber were the little rooms where the slaves who guarded the harem used to live.

Two days later we reached Oran, the naval harbour which was many years later to become famous when our fleet attacked and landed marines whilst General Montgomery advanced.

Ten miles from Tangier we heard a grinding noise in the back axle. One of the many stones in the Italian roads had pierced the axle casing, and the oil had leaked away. Our oil gauge had been put out of order by the constant vibration, or I would have known that we were losing oil. How grateful we were to have the backing of Mr Edge: he came to our rescue by sending his chief mechanic to Tangier with a new axle. Within a few hours we had found a garage and the car was towed to Tangier.

We had expected that the trip would have its problems. With

14 Shipping the car to Tangier

the new axle installed we were sure all our troubles were now over. But we had reckoned without one further bridge. After crossing the Straits of Gibraltar, we continued through Spain. For once we took things easily, and visited many interesting places in Seville and near Madrid. We had felt we must have a look at Portugal, which was on our itinerary. Passing through Badajoz we continued for about six kilometres to the Spanish frontier.

We produced our carnet and other documents – those Ali Baba had nearly pinched – and, having duly passed through the custom control, started to cross the bridge which formed the actual frontier. Now we found ourselves in real trouble. The chief customs officer on the Portuguese side pointed out that we had no visa to enter. The word on the carnet was 'Pologne', which, he explained, was Poland.

'We've come to the wrong country', I said to my passengers.

15 'We've come to the wrong country!'

We turned back over the bridge. The officials who had checked us out of Spain and stamped our carnet had gone off duty, and those now in charge refused us re-entry into Spain, because our documents now showed we had come from nowhere.

'Go back and get into Portugal', they said, 'and then check out and we will be able to pass you into Spain.' Back over the bridge we drove, but it was no use: the officials were not prepared to let us into their country without a visa. Over the bridge again we went, only to receive the same answer, that we had come from nowhere as far as they were concerned.

If it had not been so cold I think I might have seen the funny side of this affair. We were in no-man's land and it looked as though we were going to stay there for life. Further, all the arguments were taking place in Spanish and Portuguese, which made it all the more difficult.

Then a miracle happened. An Englishman arrived. He was

16 A road on the way to Madrid

very amused at the whole business, but he told me, 'Go up those stairs and knock on the door of the Chief Customs Officer'. I promptly did so, and was greeted by a charming man who spoke quite good English. He was smiling as he led me downstairs and inspected our faulty document. He scratched through the stamp which permitted us to leave Spain and wished us good luck for the rest of our journey. Feeling very cold but happy we returned to Madrid.

17 The welcome
outside the Hotel Cecil, with S.F. Edge . . .

We were not to return straight to England however: Mr Edge had suggested that we might show that the car was still in fine fettle after all its guelling journey, by running it for one thousand miles round the Montlhéry racetrack outside Paris. We aimed at an average sixty miles an hour.

This done – without problems – we made our way back to London. The press, particularly the *Daily Sketch*, showed great interest in our achievement. When I wonder why I had driven all that way without relief at the wheel, I think it was perhaps because I wanted to take the opportunity of showing how easy the AC was to drive. Perhaps, too, the press's mistaken statement at the beginning made me feel that driving single-handed was expected of me.

Whatever the reason, Mr Edge was pleased. He had arranged a lunch for us on our return, at the Hotel Cecil in the

18 . . . and at Thames Ditton

Strand. In his speech, he said, 'She's earned that little car. It's outside. I've given it to her.'

And when we drove back to the AC factory at Thames Ditton, there was a surprise waiting for us there too, a tribute which meant a great deal. All the workers, the men and women who had built the car, were waiting outside the factory to welcome us home.

Three

Furthest North

LATER on that year, one evening at our home in Esher, I opened an atlas to find out where Lapland was. With the circuit of Montlhéry still in my mind, I thought it was better actually to *go* somewhere. Also it seemed worthwhile to find out about road conditions in places we might choose as starting points for the Monte Carlo Rally. Lapland was a possibility: better than lapping Montlhéry!

I noticed, looking at the map, that the Arctic Circle ran through Finnish Lapland and Greenland. It occurred to me that no motor car had then been taken far north of the Arctic Circle anywhere in the world. Knowing how very pleased Mr Edge would be if his AC could be driven further north than any other car, I was soon in his office putting the idea to him. He was helpful as ever, and arranged for our AC to be newly painted and supplied with any necessary spares.

On 9 July 1927, therefore, Victor, Bobby Beare and I left the Hotel Cecil for the Arctic. We could obtain little information about road conditions in northern Lapland. We decided simply to drive north until we could go no further. We imagined it would be cold in the Arctic – but of course it was summer, and we struck a polar heat wave. Instead of being frost-bitten, we were mosquito-bitten.

Having crossed the English Channel, we made our way through France, Belgium, Holland and Germany to Denmark.

We all loved Holland. Many roads were bordered by closely set trees, which made it seem that we were driving through a luminous green tunnel. The tulips were in full bloom, too, and this part of our journey was a pleasure.

We were due to call for letters in Hamburg, but slowed down

by fog, we did not do so, which was a pity: waiting for us was a letter from Copenhagen, stating that an audience had been arranged for us with King Christian of Denmark. His Majesty had heard, it seemed, of our Arctic adventure, and wished to learn more about it from us personally.

On our way to Copenhagen we passed through several villages and at every garage mechanics waved, trying to stop us. Victor, however, would have none of it. He kept saying, 'Take no notice. They're only trying to sell us a fog lamp.'

He was wrong. Messages from the Palace had been sent to every garage along the route, because it was realised that we had not called at the Post Office in Hamburg. We arrived at our hotel in Copenhagen, still happily unaware that we had sped past a chain of Royal Commands. Soon after the arrival the British Ambassador called. He was very concerned, and told us we had missed an audience with King Christian. He doubted whether His Majesty would honour us with another appointment. But he too was wrong. The Palace was soon in touch with him. The King would be pleased to grant us an audience the next day.

So at 2.30 the following afternoon we were ushered into the Royal presence. The King showed great interest in our Monte Carlo adventures, and we discussed them as well as our immediate plans, for some time.

That night, a dinner and ball was held in our honour, attended by Prince Harold, the brother of King Christian, and Princess Helene, grand-daughter of Queen Victoria. As we entered the ballroom the band played the British national anthem followed by the Danish national anthem. It was a moving experience as we stood to attention.

We stayed only one night in Copenhagen because of the long journey which lay before us to the Arctic Circle. Two days later we reached Sweden, Stockholm being our next stay. We found driving through the forest most fascinating. All the trees were so well cared for. We were welcomed by the President and a number of members of the Royal Swedish Automobile Club. They showed great enthusiasm over our plan to drive to the

19 In the Finnish forest

Arctic Circle. They advised us to follow the coast road to the frontier between Sweden and Finland. We were not able to learn much about the roads in northern Finland.

People back home thought, I suppose, that we were spending our nights in igloos: most of the time we were a good deal more comfortable than they imagined, apart, of course, from that polar heatwave and the forest fire we were soon to meet. Naturally I did nothing to disillusion them when we got home. I didn't tell them, for instance, that not far from the Arctic Circle I found a hairdresser as good as any I'd known in London, Paris or New York. Before I'd left I'd had my hair bobbed in Bond Street. Shingling was more fashionable at the time, but I preferred the bob. When the Arctic hairdresser saw me, however, he moaned, 'Madam! Who has done that to your hair?'

Almost apologetically I told him I'd been to one of the best salons in London. He shook his head in despair, and gave me one of the finest shingles I'd ever seen.

At Haparanda, on the Sweden–Finland border, we drove over a narrow wooden bridge that spanned the River Tornio. We saw a big notice, but we couldn't understand it because it

20 The bridge at Tornio

was in Swedish. It was only when we reached the other side that we learned what it said. Horrified locals who had watched us explained that it was there to warn everyone that the bridge was under construction and unsafe even for pedestrians. We'd gone over it so fast, it seems, that we didn't give it time to collapse!

Just a few miles south of the Arctic Circle, we ran into a storm, and we could see in the distance that the lightning had set fire to the forest. As we neared, we could see that the flames were leaping above the trees: they must have been over a hundred feet high. We could feel the heat, and the front was moving towards us. By now, reindeer were galloping across in front of us: we guessed that, by instinct, they were making for water. The fire was still a few miles away, but we knew we should follow the animals' example. Our map showed that there was a lake a little way off our track, confirming that the animals knew where they were going.

We reached in the lake in twenty minutes, and at last could relax in comparative safety. Some previous fire, by great good fortune, had burnt the woodland around the shores, and this made a natural fire-break. We were to feel the heat grow yet much greater, but could watch the grandeur of the flames in the safety of the burnt strip, with the water near if need be. There must have been hundreds of reindeer, and thousands of smaller animals, by the lakeside with us.

It was over five hours before the fire died down.

We then continued driving north – initially over the fire ravaged land. Eventually, we ran out of road: the wood gradually thickened to forest, and we knew we could continue little further. For a little way, we cut down the trees which prevented our going further, but before much longer, there were too many, and we had to stop.

We planted the Union Jack about two hundred and fifty miles north of the Arctic Circle, and about forty from the Arctic Ocean. No motor car had ever been so near the North Pole before, and even these days, I doubt that there's what you'd call a traffic jam up there.

On the return journey, having accomplished the task we had set ourselves, we took our time exploring the fairyland of Sweden. It was then that we saw our only wolf: it was stuffed! The press in England had not realised that our journey north was in summer, and wrote accounts of our adventure which implied that we were constantly in danger from snow, or bitter cold, or wolves. We were in fact to have rather more trouble with snow when we were in Poland.

Returning to Tornio, the Finnish town on the other side of the river from Haparanda, we enquired if there was a bridge more suitable than that we had used going the other way. We had to go some twenty miles from Tornio, but it was worth it to cross in safety.

Having left Finland, that beautiful country of a thousand lakes, we spent two nights driving by the light of the midnight sun. The roads in Sweden were smooth and well-kept and it was a joy to be able to drive the car again at forty miles an hour instead of ten miles an hour, as in Italy and northern Finland.

On reaching Sundsvall again we were welcomed by the Secretary of the Royal Swedish Automobile Club. We told him we hoped to make Sundsvall our starting point in the next Monte Carlo Rally. Before we left he gave us special maps, and also told us that the snow ploughs always kept the roads clear. A few days later we arrived back in London. A week later the Automobile Association presented us with a silver plaque sent by the Royal Swedish Automobile Club in memory of our journey through Sweden.

Four

Ten Days and Ten Nights

THROUGHOUT the late twenties and well into the thirties I was constantly busy planning to break more records. The win in the Monte Carlo Rally and my success in the Arctic further encouraged me to scan the horizon for new adventures. By the middle of October 1927, I had found a hurdle which seemed high enough and dangerous enough to merit attention. From a newspaper report I learned that a team using a Chrysler car had driven round an American track for about a week, covering 10,000 miles at a speed of over 60 m.p.h. and breaking a number of world records. A little later I heard that drivers from the Sunbeam Company were planning to attack those records in the spring of 1928. I consulted Victor, and as he also loved the racing track, we agreed to drive jointly before the year was out, and before the Sunbeam team could turn a wheel.

First I went to see Mr Edge, who had given me the AC car after the Monte Carlo Rally. I told him that I would like to break all the long distance records held by America. He was very interested, having been a racing driver himself. As I mentioned, he himself had created a 24-hour record at Brooklands in 1907, without a co-driver, averaging over 60 m.p.h.. He had told me that his car had torn great chunks out of the track. Workmen had to dash out to repair it as soon as he flashed by and before he came roaring round again.

He told me it would take time to hot up the car and arrange different springing, which meant it might not be possible to make the attempt until nearly Christmas – certainly not a good time, with weather conditions likely to be bad. But rather than run the risk of the records being raised by the Sunbeam drivers,

I planned to take the AC to the French race track Montlhéry near Paris, where one was allowed to drive day and night. I knew that it was not permitted to drive at night at Brooklands. Some years before, the local residents had raised a petition about the noise from open exhausts keeping them awake. So all-night driving was banned.

21 The Montlhéry track

Montlhéry is an egg-shaped track only a mile and a quarter round, with very steep banking. It was very expensive, because the price of the track included the time keepers. Mr Edge was unable to help us with the cost of the track because his finances like many other motor firms then, were not too good.

'I can hot up the car, and lend you my chief designer Sydney Smith, and six mechanics', he said. 'But the motor industry is going through a very bad time just now. Sales are falling drastically. I'm afraid you'll have to pay for shipping the car to France, for petrol, and for the track. I'd help you if I could.'

I was thoroughly grateful for what he was able to offer, and supremely confident as usual that in some way or another we could raise the extra funds needed. First Victor tried approaching his trustees for an advance; but when they learned how he planned to spend it they refused to have anything to do with the enterprise. It was much too great a risk, they said, financially, and in every other way.

So I decided to try to penetrate the defences of my trustee, a solicitor who held my Aunt Maud's legacy in trust for me. At four o'clock one day I called at his London office. I told him with glowing enthusiasm of my plan to bring glory to the family, to the British motor car industry, to Britain itself. He waited until I paused for breath and then he said, 'Your aunt settled this money in trust for you on condition that you spend it wisely. I regret that I cannot regard the enterprise you contemplate as wise.'

I had expected that cautious reply and was ready to counter-attack with a wide variety of weapons. I pleaded, argued, demanded and got cross; but it was no good. After an hour he said he was going home for his tea. I told him I'd wait. About six o'clock he came back and said, 'Good gracious! Don't tell me you're still here! And sitting in the same position too!' I said nothing; I continued to sit in the same position. Then to my utter joy he heaved a sigh and said, 'I suppose I shall have to advise your aunt to release some of the trust money, though where this determination of yours will lead you, goodness only knows. Anyhow . . . Good luck!'

Jubilantly I left his office. The price of the track, £250, had been secured. The cost of getting the car across the channel in those days was only £2 10s. and petrol was just tenpence a gallon. Back I went to Mr Edge to tell him the news and to ask him if he could start getting the car ready.

Basically the AC was an ordinary open sports car. The mechanics took off the mudguards for extra streamlining, making it look like a wasp without wings. Then they fitted a special axle to make it high-geared and finally they tuned the engine. Neither Victor nor I test-drove it, because we knew the car well from our Monte Carlo experiences. Furthermore, we had complete faith in the experts who were preparing it for us, particularly in Sydney Smith, the chief designer.

I shall always remember him with affection and respect. He was a remarkable man, and a brilliant designer. He designed the first 'light six', an aluminium six-cylinder engine that was about ten years ahead of its time. The very fact that he was going to be in the pits when we made our attempt on all those records gave us confidence, because he wasn't just a genius, but an old friend.

The night before we left England I wrote to my mother: 'Victor and I are going to France for ten days. We're going to drive through the world and back again. Haven't time to write any more now, but you'll probably read all about it in the newspapers. . . . '

Whenever I was on the verge of any exploit or escapade like that I always wrote to Mama and broke the news to her as gently as possible. I never wanted to worry her because she was very emotional, always quite sure I was going to kill myself. So I used to try and make it all sound easy and I always wrote at the last minute so that she wouldn't have a chance to say, 'Don't do it!' She probably had no idea of what I meant when I wrote about going through the world and back again, but that was the distance we hoped to cover – some 15,000 miles.

We drove the car from the AC works in Thames Ditton, Surrey, to the cross-Channel boat. Sydney Smith and the six mechanics came, too, and so did S.F. Edge, who planned to stay in Montlhéry for the first two days of the record attempt. The entire party had booked into a hotel called Château Montlhéry about a mile from the race track. It was a beautiful three-storey gabled building, built of timber, a second home for the racing drivers who came to Montlhéry from all over the world.

The heart of the hotel was Madame Patrice, who ran it with her husband. She was about forty-five years old, plump and always cheerful. She understood people who lived dangerously and was very close to us all, the great names as well as those scarcely known. She feared for us all, too, but was too wise to show that fear, let alone express it. She had known her friends triumph on that track which she seldom visited, and she had known them killed there. No matter what happened, she carried on with the job she loved: looking after racing motorists. She was like a mother to us.

When she died the drivers who knew her did not forget her. On the track at Montlhéry there is a memorial to two great personalities of the era. The inscription on it reads: 'To Bignan who died in Belsen Camp and to Madame Patrice who helped us all'. Bignan was a great Italian ace who used to drive a single-seater Amilcar brilliantly. Madame Patrice knew him well. She would have understood the irony of a man who risked his life so often in the name of sport, dying in the squalor of a Nazi concentration camp; and Bignan would have understood why her name was linked with his on that memorial. She was part of motor racing, part of our lives.

My first meeting with Madame Patrice was delayed by an element which we could both have done without. The AC party arrived in the neighbourhood of Montlhéry on the afternoon of 8 December 1927 in dense fog, and it took them an hour and a half to find the Château. Madame Patrice made us welcome immediately; but one of the guests did little to raise our spirits.

We went into the dining room at six o'clock that evening for supper. There we met this chap who had been testing a motor cycle on the track. When he heard why we were there, he said gloomily, 'I suppose you know we've had thick fog here for two weeks. When do you hope to start driving?'

I said, 'Tomorrow evening at seven o'clock.' Even more gloomily he replied, 'What are you going to do if it's still foggy?'

'Drive full out just the same', I told him; and that was what we did.

The following morning we went to the track. Not only was it foggy and getting foggier, but it was freezing cold. Because our attempt at the record had to be recognised officially, twelve time-keepers from the Automobile Club of France were there and we went to their control hut to sign on as soon as we arrived.

The chief time-keeper looked at us curiously. Then he said, 'Where are the other drivers?'

'There aren't any others', I told him. 'Only us.' There was silence for a moment. Then they looked at each other and began to smile. I don't speak French very fluently, but I heard one murmur to his colleagues, 'Mon Dieu, we'll be out of here by tomorrow.'

He meant, of course, that in those conditions, fog and freezing cold, the coldest winter on record, we did not have a chance. I must admit that the outlook didn't look too bright for us.

Still, we were there to drive, and drive we would. After we'd signed on we went out to the car and watched the mechanics fussing round the engine. They're a breed of their own, racing mechanics. Any engine they tune becomes a personal possession, and woe betide any driver who blows it up. The mechanic always blames the driver, never the engine. If they could find a car which did not need a driver, they would be happy!

22 In the AC on the Montlhéry track

When they were satisfied at last I drove a trial lap to get the feel of the track. At once I found it was very different from Brooklands. It was much smaller, of course, only a mile and a quarter round. As I went high on the banking, I felt as if the track was bearing down on me. It was like that well-known fair-ground act, the Wall of Death, and it made me feel dizzy, almost sick.

Then it was Victor's turn for a trial run. I said nothing to him or to anyone else about the strange dizzy sensation I had known because I felt it would pass in time; and when he had finished his run he was quiet, too. He probably had had the same sensation, but kept quiet about it in case it worried me.

We had decided to drive in relays of three hours each. We tossed to see who would start, and I won. Sharp at seven o'clock that evening I set off on the first lap and by that time the fog was getting really bad, settling down solidly on the track. The headlights had been taken off the car, not to lighten it but because on a heavily banked track they could not reach the top or bottom of it and were useless. Instead there were hurricane lamps placed every four yards round the perimeter and by nine o'clock the fog was so thick that I could see only about five lamps ahead.

I knew that we were going to face conditions like that for quite a while. All I could do was keep my foot down and drive by feel. On a banked track, it is possible to feel quite accurately where one is. There is less guide on the straights, of course, as they are flat. But Montlhéry had no very long straights, and at least I had a few lamps to guide me. I had started, and I had to carry on now, or abandon the attempt.

At the end of three hours, I had to go into the pits: stopping accurately in the pits after travelling at such speed was not easy in the fog. Coming in for the first time, I overshot, and had to go straight out at the far end; but soon I learnt where to take off the power, and could stop accurately. Time was of the essence in the pits. The chief engineer would have his stop watch out, noting exactly how long each take-over and refuelling took. At that first change-over, Victor was in the car and away in less than two and three-quarter minutes; I left for the Château to snatch what sleep I could in three hours. My eyes ached from the intense peering into the fog, I was physically tired out by the driving, and the bumps every few seconds made it even more exhausting. (Not even the best tracks are smooth at such speed.) I was, at least, a little cheered by the news that I had averaged eighty miles an hour for those first three hours.

Back at the Château Madame Patrice tried to tempt me to eat with a delicious plate of scrambled eggs mixed with cheese, but I was too exhausted to face it. I just fell into bed and in what seemed like minutes she was shaking my shoulder, telling me it was time to get up again. On the dot of one o'clock in the morning I was back at the wheel to find that the track was freezing. For the next ten days and ten nights that was how we spent our lives. While one slept, the other hurled that little AC car round the steep, egg-shaped track, first through thick fog and later over black ice, at up to 95 m.p.h. By the fourth day the fog had finally cleared, but the temperature plunged below zero. We had no time to talk and we could not have heard each other anyway, because the roar of the engine hour after hour left us more or less deaf. Instead we wrote each other little notes in the Château: 'Fog clearing' or 'Black ice' or 'Watch out for the big bump on the banking half-way from the pits'. That was the bump that I was to discuss forty-seven years later at Silverstone with Peter Wardle.

After three days and nights we had a welcome visitor who later was to save us from severe injury. He was Dr Receau from Paris, a motor racing enthusiast and once a competitive driver himself. He had heard of our record attempt and had come out to the track to offer any help he could.

By that time we had decided that three hours' sleep was not enough. We extended the driving shift to six hours which gave us longer sleep and a chance to recharge our batteries of mind and body. We would pull up at the pits, absolutely freezing after driving continuously for six hours, though it didn't make much difference to our performance. We became part of the car, sitting there in misery for hours that seemed to go on forever. A real danger, of course, was frost-bite, when we extended the number of hours from three to six. In fact we did get frost-bitten fingers, and I have the scars on two of them to this day.

Luckily Dr Receau solved this problem for us before it became really dangerous. Had he not done so, we could each have lost a few fingers. The medicine he gave us would not be found in any medical book, but it worked. He told Sydney Smith to massage our fingers with warm oil. It worked faster than warm water and for some reason or other the pain was less severe.

Cold and lack of sleep were two of our worst enemies. The worst time was just before the dawn when everyone is at the lowest ebb. I had to fight all the way to keep awake and the unbelievable monotony of the constant circling, lap after lap after lap, was not much help. Even the constant noise of the engine was almost hypnotising.

As we continued this seemingly endless journey, it grew colder and colder. We created our own blizzard by travelling so fast in the freezing air. Then nature added a blizzard of her own. Ice began accumulating on the windscreen, and we had no wipers because at the speed we were travelling they would have been whipped off the car. We had to keeping peering over the top of the windscreen into the driving sleet until I invented a piece of equipment that today is used on race tracks all over the world: the vizor.

I thought of the idea in the Château. Someone brought me some celluloid and I made one there and then in Madame Patrice's dining room while my scrambled eggs got cold. That vizor meant that we could move the windscreen down a bit and get a glimpse of the track and the hurricane lamps. If we'd done nothing else on that nightmare drive, we at least gave something to future drivers. The trouble was that our breath condensed in it and formed icicles. Soon the car was covered in icicles, too.

Ironically it was this brutal cold which saved us from failure. On the third day when I pulled up at the pits to refuel, Sydney Smith saw a huge icicle hanging from the radiator and said. 'Thank God for the blizzard! There's a leak in the radiator and the ice is sealing it. If it starts to thaw, we're beaten.' There I was praying for the cold to go while Sydney was praying it would stay. But he was a wonderful man, very sympathetic. He was very worried about this no sleep business and it was he who suggested we should do six- instead of three-hour shifts.

On the fifth day the French Press began to take an interest in our marathon journey. On the sixth, a fair number of Parisians made their way to the track to watch us. Until then they had been huddling over their home fires because they could not stand on the ice-bound pavements. They were just in time to see us break the 10,000 mile record, a landmark which we failed to appreciate fully because we were too dazed by fatigue, our minds virtually numbed by cold.

That sixth day, however, had a dramatically sombre side, too. It is true that we had achieved already one of our major objects, the 10,000 mile record, and that Paris was saluting us, but in addition we had four exceptionally unwelcome visitors.

Madame Patrice woke me up when I was in the middle of a beautiful sleep and long before I was due to get up. She looked very worried and said, 'There are some gentlemen down in the hall talking to Mr Smith, and there seems to be trouble. I think you'd better go down.'

I looked at the clock and saw that I wasn't due to drive for another two hours. Nevertheless I dressed quickly, and went down to find Sydney deep in argument with four men wearing berets. They were talking very fast and looked very angry. I said to Sydney, 'What's wrong? I know it's something about money, but they're talking too quickly for me to understand.'

He told me quietly, 'It seems the owner of the track went bankrupt a little while ago and it was taken over by the liquidators. You paid the ex-owner instead of the liquidators and now they're here, looking for £250.'

I was furious. 'Another £250!' I said. 'Pay all over again? Never!' I didn't bother to add that I hadn't got it anyway. Sydney explained to the men in berets my strong view of the affair. They shrugged their shoulders and said, 'Unless we get £250, we'll put up barriers across the track.'

Sydney, who spoke excellent French, relayed their ultimatum to me. By that time I was shaking with cold, misery and exhaustion and almost crying with frustration. Grimly I said to Sydney, 'Tell them nothing's going to stop me now. I'll drive through their barriers!'

He turned to them again and the argument resumed. At first it was as heated as ever, but gradually it became more reasonable and from the snatches I could understand I could see that we were winning. At last, after what seemed like a century, a dark age, the four men began smiling. They shook hands with Sydney, with me and with Madame Patrice, who had been hovering anxiously on the fringe of it all. Then they bowed to us and left, wishing us luck. I said to Sydney, 'Quickly . . . tell me what's happening.'

With a broad smile he said, 'The French are great sportsmen. I told them you'd been frozen out there on the track for six days and nights, but in spite of that had broken over a dozen records. I said it would be tragic if they interfered with the drive now when you were on the verge of making motoring history.'

'And they accepted that?' I said. 'Was that all you had to say? It seemed to take a long time.'

His smile grew even broader. 'Actually I said a little more', he told me. 'I made it quite clear that I had known you for a long time, and was quite certain that you would drive through any barriers they erected. At first they didn't believe me, but when I told them about your Monte Carlo record they changed their minds.'

Weak with relief, I went back to bed to have the half-hour of sleep that was left to me after the interruption.

The seventh night brought an even more serious crisis. By then the track was like glass. Nobody could stand on it. Driving at ten miles an hour would have been dangerous and we were topping ninety-five. As I got out of the car I shouted to Victor, 'Solid black ice!' Then I nearly fell on the ice by the pits. The mechanics nearly fell, too, dashing to fill the tank; and out on the track it was worse. The bumps caused wheel spin. Every time I hit a bad one, a tyre left the ground for a split second and when it landed it spun – that could send the car spinning, too.

I was lucky . . . I must have hit the bumps evenly; the car never tried to turn over when I was driving it. At that speed, if the car tipped and skidded I could have done nothing to save it. Victor must have caught only one wheel on a bump. At midnight, he came into the bedroom and woke me. He was covered in oil. Horrified, I said, 'Has it blown up? Don't tell me the engine's gone?' With a smile he said, 'The engine's fine. I've been underneath the car, that's all.'

I was so thankful to see he was unhurt and to learn the car was all right, though obviously we were in trouble. He sat on the bed and told me he'd hit that big bump half way to the pits. The car had skidded on the ice, turned round several times, dived off the track into the mud and turned upside down. It had slid along on its back for a while and finally stopped with him underneath. By the grace of God the steering wheel hadn't broken, and this had stopped the weight of the car from crushing him.

For the second night running I had dressed quickly, hours before I was due to get up. We had work to do. The French Automobile Club rules stated that no work could be done on the car except at the pits and that nobody was allowed to help us move the car on the track. All the mechanics and spectators were allowed to do was to lift the car off Victor and get it back on its wheels.

To get it out of the mud onto the track was our job, and it took the pair of us two hours. We were only six yards from the track, but we could only move it inch by inch, shoving and hauling furiously. The others had to watch, yearning to help, but knowing we'd be disqualified if they as much as laid a finger on the car.

Once we had it back on the track we had to push it about half a mile to the pits, but that was easy compared with getting back on to the track. The mechanics went to work at once. They told us the steering had been badly damaged and the windscreen torn off, but they were fairly sure they could get it back on the job again in twelve hours.

Those hours were precious, but luckily we were well ahead of schedule and still could capture a few more records. They fixed the steering, but could do nothing about the windscreen because we had brought no replacement. So Sydney Smith fixed a number plate where the screen should have been. That gave us some protection, and stopped the blizzard blowing our heads backwards, though we had to peer over the top of it, of course.

By that time it was colder than ever. We had two days left to catch up on our average speed, which now had dropped to 65 m.p.h. We both knew we'd have to drive all-out for those remaining forty-eight hours and, my goodness, I did admire Victor's pluck, getting back into that car after it had nearly killed him. Making matters worse, Sydney Smith, our tower of strength, got pneumonia. He kept on working, which was typical of him, but in the end he simply collapsed and *had* to go to bed.

Then came the final scare. Snow was forecast. We'd been able to handle the sleety blizzard and could manage the black ice. A heavy snow fall, however, would have finished us. So we just had to pray that it would hold off for another few hours.

Our prayers were answered . . . or very nearly answered. The snow began on the tenth day, two hours before our final lap. I was driving and just kept going as fast as that little AC could manage. The drifts were building up in crevices beside the track, but soon I saw a sight that made me forget them. As I flashed by the pits, the chief engineer held up a board with a huge number 10 on it. Ten laps to go! The snow was blinding now, but on I went, watching those numbers diminish each time I passed the pits – *9 . . . 8 . . . 7 . . . 6 . . . 5 . . . 4 . . . 3 . . . 2 . . . 1*. Even the mechanics and the time-keepers were cheering as I made that final lap and clambered out of the car.

A huge crowd had gathered at the track by that time. I remember Victor and I being hugged by a cheering band of total strangers. Some had brought wreaths of flowers which they put round our necks. Where they got them at that time of the year and in that weather, heaven knows! Then, exhausted but delighted, we made our way to the time-keeper's office. There we learned we had broken seventeen world records right up to 15,000 miles at an average speed of 68 miles an hour. I had written to my mother that we were going to drive through the world and back again and we had done it – but only just in

23 The last of thirteen thousand laps begins

time: two hours later the track was buried under three feet of snow.

We returned to the Chateau Montlhéry where Madame Patrice was waiting to congratulate us. As usual we were too tired to eat. Rest was the first reward we wanted; and ironically even that was to be denied us because we had one more crisis to face.

We all went to bed that night, dead beat. At last we were warm. Unfortunately it soon became too warm. At about two o'clock in the morning, Victor jumped up and shouted, 'We're on fire!' He opened the door and smoke poured into the room. He shouted to me, 'Tie sheets together.' Then he wrapped a wet towel round his head and dashed off to see what he could do about it. He closed the door behind him to stop the smoke coming in as I began tying the sheets together. There were only four of them; I hung them out the window, but the end was at least twenty feet from the ground. There were no blankets, just

24 The welcome at the end of ten days' and ten nights' driving

a couple of eiderdowns. Have you ever tried tying two eiderdowns together? It's a hopeless task. I managed it somehow, but they added only a couple of feet between them to our life-line, which still dangled many feet from the ground. Really, it was quite ridiculous. For days we'd been nearly frozen to death. Now it seemed as if we were going to burn to death.

Madame Patrice was leaning out of the top floor window shouting in French that she was going to jump. Luckily Victor came dashing back, the wet towel still round his head, and shouted up to her, 'Non, non! Très bien . . . très bien!' He spoke a little French. Then he told me what had happened. One of the mechanics had fallen asleep in bed, exhausted, with a cigarette in his hand. It had set fire to the hair mattress, which made a lot of smoke, but not much fire. Victor pulled him out of bed, opened a window and then threw the mechanic into a cold bath. After that he dealt with the mattress. It really was exciting, and most of the others missed it. Madame Patrice and the mechanic and Victor and I were the only people who knew about the fire. The rest of them slept soundly through all the commotion.

Looking back, the whole business doesn't surprise me. I was born on 10 November under the sign of Scorpio. My mother had always told me that frightful things were constantly nearly happening to Scorpios . . . but never more than nearly!

The French Automobile Club gave us a special luncheon to commemorate our achievement, at which they presented us with a gold plaque inscribed 'L'Automobile-Club de France à L'Honorable Victor Bruce et Mrs Bruce. Records du Monde de 4000 à 15000 milles, Autodrome de Linas, Montlhéry, 9-19 Décembre, 1927.'

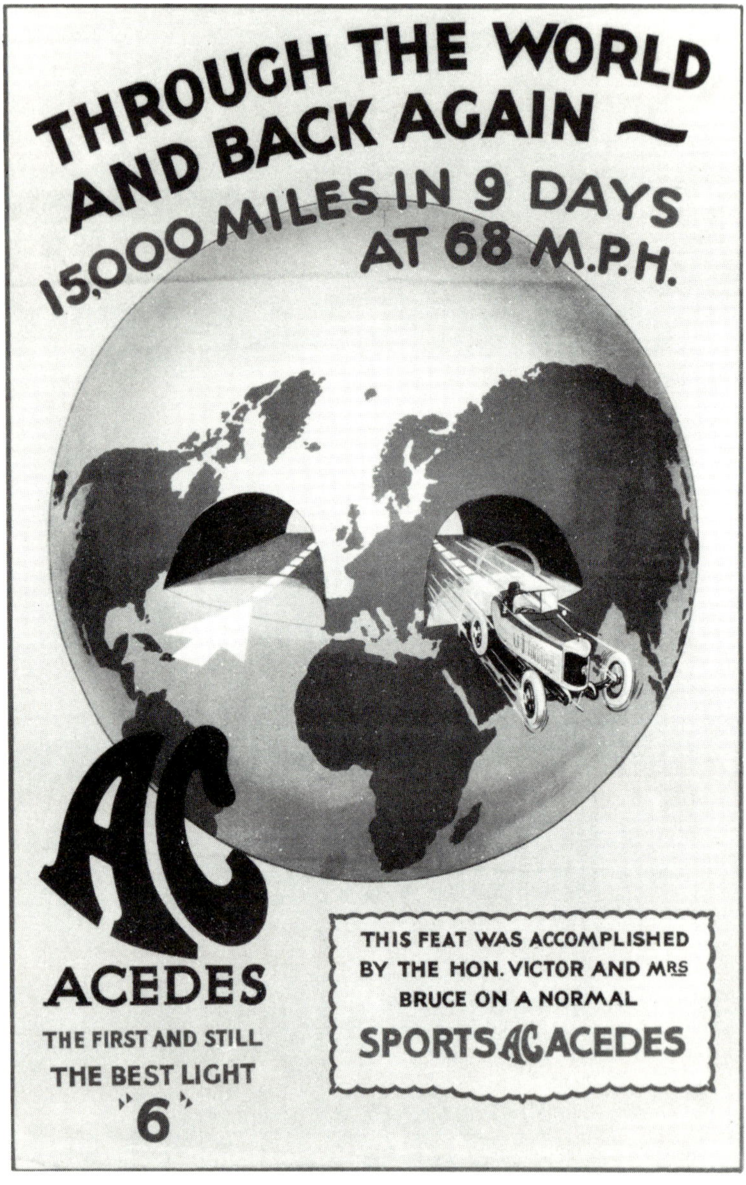

26 A contemporary poster for AC cars reported the event

Five

Brooklands and More

My continued partnership with the AC car firm led to Mr Edge letting me drive his special racing car *Tiny Tim*. It had terrific acceleration, and held the record for a standing-start half mile.

Someone suggested that I drive it up the Brooklands test hill. Little did I know what was going to happen to me at the top. The hill was 1 in 4. Having driven up at top speed, the car took off at the top, only by good fortune landing on all fours. I disappointed the photographers who wanted me to repeat this performance by deciding not to risk it again.

I well remember my first race at Brooklands. It was for the Surbiton Cup, a touring-car race. One of my competitors was the famous driver Frazer-Nash. On that occasion, I managed to beat him by a short bonnet. As I passed him, he called out, 'You'll blow that crate up one of these days!'

How right he was. It wasn't in the race, though. In the excitement of winning, I did an extra lap. That additional lap ran an engine bearing dry, and I had to avoid the chief engineer for a while afterwards, as he was not best pleased.

I spent much of 1928 racing at Brooklands, or on the sands near Blackpool, where regular races had started a few years previously. Sand racing was great fun, but one had to take care because cornering too quickly caused a pile of sand to mount up, and the car could hit it and turn over.

Still in my AC, it was about now that I entered a most exciting event called the Alpine Trial. It was called a trial, but in reality was more of a road race. It was run from Milan to Munich over the Alps, a distance of eleven hundred miles.

In order to have a chance of winning, one had to average over thirty miles an hour, and that required flat-out driving where ever possible. On the second day of the five-day race, a car with a photographer came alongside ours just as the road narrowed. We collided. A rock, jutting out into the road, caught my front wheel, and our speed of seventy miles an hour was rapidly reduced to nothing. We came to rest teetering on the edge of the mountainside.

A wheel was following the car. Seeing it, I said to Victor, 'We've lost our spare wheel.'

'Spare be blowed! It's our front wheel.'

We were towed down the hill to the village, where repairs were carried out within an hour; we were soon away again. We finished the day's run on time, and recorded the fastest total. Because we had not done the repairs ourselves, we were not given the Alpine Cup. But the Club recognised our achievement, and gave us a special medal instead.

It was not long after this that I was approached by another car manufacturer, the Alvis Company, and asked if I would like to join their works team. I said 'Yes' at once, because I knew it would give me the chance of competing against the giants of the racing drivers of the day. I was able to drive the Alvis in the 'double twelve' two-day race at Brooklands. John Cobb was in the team, and Malcolm Campbell, in another make of car, was one of our rivals. To make the event more exciting for spectators, sand banks were put up in the finishing straight, to act as artificial corners. There were no problems until the second day, when three Talbot cars collided just as they were passing the spectators' enclosure. One overturned and went into the crowd. It was the worst crash ever on an English racetrack. There is a legend that the ghost of one of the drivers, in old-fashioned kit, is seen occasionally near the site of the crash.

The race was not stopped after the crash, because the organisers knew that if they did cancel the remaining laps, everyone would start going home, and the ambulances would be unable to get through. It was a miserable day for all of us, but I had some consolation in finishing first in my class.

It was also at Brooklands that I raced with Sir Henry

Segrave, a true professional who nearly always finished a race, and frequently won. He used to give me advice: 'Stop broadsiding round the corners. You may save a few minutes on the circuit, but you'll lose a lot more in the pits changing the tyres.'

Brooklands is today no more, but I shall remember the track: it was two-and-a-half miles round, and very bumpy at high speed. In one race, my dashboard split and the steering dropped down. But as usual, even when my car came to grief, I survived. Something similar happened in the 1929 Monte Carlo Rally.

The AC was damaged in a car park just before we were due to set out for our chosen starting point in the 1929 Rally. There was no time to get it mended, so we arranged with the Arrol Company in Scotland to use one of their Arrol-Asters in the Rally.

We had chosen as our starting place Riga in Latvia, because of the extra marks for distance. We encountered the worst weather possible. From Germany northwards, it snowed without a break. We were within six miles of the Polish border when we were stopped by a snowdrift. The car slipped into a ditch. A blizzard was blowing and the temperature was about twenty degrees below zero. Somehow Victor managed to let the water out of the radiator. Unfortunately the last village we passed was some three miles back. We knew that if we did not get shelter we would be frozen to death. So we started to walk.

After only a mile I wanted to sit down and rest because I felt sleepy. This does happen when you are exposed to extreme cold, but it is fatal to rest. So continuing, some two or three miles later, we at last saw a light and reached a small hut on the outskirts of the village we had driven through. A man opened the door, but I think he thought we were gipsies, for he began to close the door on us. We showed him the mascot which we had taken off the car for safety. He then opened the door again, let us in and lit a fire. After a while with a little bit of German I had learnt at school he began to understand what had happened to us.

The next morning he arranged for us to hire two sleigh

horses, and with some rope we all returned to the car. But it was nearly buried by the heavy snow fall: just the top stuck out through the snow. With difficulty we managed to pull the car back on to the road, and towed by the two sleigh horses we

27 'We managed to pull the car back onto the road.'
Snowdrifts near the Polish border.

reached a railway station. The car in due course arrived in Berlin, where we received by telegram the Club's permission to restart. The rules laid down by the Monaco Club permitted competitors, if they could not reach their scheduled starting point due to roads being closed, to start from the nearest town where there would be a Club official to see them off.

We were not very happy about the wiring, as one of the lights appeared to flicker, but there was no time to overhaul the car because the other competitors had already started when we reached Berlin. Nevertheless we caught them all up in Paris, and all went well from there onwards. We made a fast journey, but within six miles of Avignon, just before dawn, all the lights went out, and smoke began to pour out of the bonnet. The car was on fire, and there was little we could do.

Our small fire extinguisher saved a complete disaster, and the loss of the car, but the wiring had completely burnt out: the snow had caused a short-circuit.

We all returned sadly home – by train.

From our experience near the Polish border in this 1929 Rally, I had learned that a very large car was unsuitable. With a crew of four it was possible to lift a small car out of a ditch should we be unfortunate enough to slide off the ice-bound roads. So for 1930, we chose a Hillman straight-eight saloon, with seating for three passengers.

In 1930 competitors were still allowed by the Monaco Club to select their starting point. With the experience gained during our journey beyond the Arctic Circle, we decided to start from Sundsvall half way up Sweden, 2,200 miles from Monte Carlo.

We left London in the middle of January for our starting point. We were prepared to struggle through deep snow when we reached Sweden, but we were not expecting the unfortunate accident about twenty miles from Sundsvall. I had just handed over the wheel to one of my co-drivers when we struck a very bad patch of ice coming down a steep hill. The car took charge and I realised nothing could save an accident. It was dark too, and we gathered speed bouncing from side to side, finally hitting an enormous rock, and leaping off the road. We came to rest on two more rocks. We were uninjured except for a few bruises, but it looked as though the car was finished. By the light of a torch we started to examine the damage, but to our joy and astonishment only the tool box and exhaust pipe were broken. How to get the car back on the road was the problem.

As we waited beside the road hoping some car would appear, a lorry drew up. Luckily the driver had some rope, and appeared used to pulling cars when they had left the road. Within half an hour he had the Hillman back on the road. We were most grateful for the lorry driver's help, and were soon finishing the twenty miles to Sundsvall. We were amazed at the readiness, almost joy, with which a small garage in Sundsvall set about repairing our car. Everything was completed by the dawn, and on the stroke of eight o'clock the starter appointed by the Automobile Club of Sweden flagged us off. Our route through the town was lined with spectators, and on various points on the way back to Stockholm villagers had turned out; some presented us with bouquets. They all realised that we were on our way to Monte Carlo because of the rally plate fixed to the car.

Conditions right down to Stockholm were very trying, chiefly because heavy snow was falling, and ice-bound roads were a special hazard. Nevertheless we reached Stockholm safely.

There was no time to linger: there never is in the Monte Carlo Rally, and it was then necessary to average about forty-three miles an hour in order to arrive at the various check points on time. Marks are lost for every minute one is late. The rest of the journey through Denmark, Belgium and France was one mighty dash, with no time to stop even for a meal. But the excitement kept me going, as I imagine it did my three passengers, who were splendid throughout. We reached Monte Carlo dead on time, and discovered we had come 480 miles further than any of the other competitors. Of course we were sure we had won, until the results were displayed the following morning. To our amazement a competitor from northern Greece had won. He had carried an extra passenger in his tiny saloon thereby gaining extra marks, and by arranging the seating with one passenger sitting on a seat fixed to the door, got round the rules regarding width of seat and feet room. It was disappointing for us all, but we had proved our British car to be a winner, even if without a prize!

Six

24 Hours at Montlhéry

IN THE meantime, on 5 June 1929, I had returned to Montlhéry, and once again stood in the pits beside the little egg-shaped track. I was about to make an attempt on the world record for single-handed driving for twenty-four hours; this time my car was not a little AC sports model, but a huge 4½-litre Bentley. Most people in the motor racing world thought that I would never do it, and all but a few thought I was crazy to try. But I was not geared to absorb words of pessimism.

The idea of attempting to break this record had not come to me overnight. Ever since my old friend S. F. Edge of the AC Company had told me how he had created a record in 1907, the thought of the challenge had lurked in my mind. When Thomas Gillett broke Edge's record in the same car some time later, averaging 80 m.p.h. for twenty-four hours without a co-driver, I decided that the time had come for me to unveil that thought, and transform it into action.

As usual there were problems, and as usual I was quite confident that I could solve them quickly, if not easily. First I had to have a car, a matter which I raised with S. F. Edge, whom I had known over the years as a thoroughly generous and helpful man. It was typical of his generosity that he had lent his own car to Thomas Gillett so that he could break the record he himself had set in 1907.

At the AC works, however, I faced my first set-back. S. F. Edge said that the AC could not be hotted up any further, certainly not sufficiently to take the record. Making matters even more gloomy, he was in poor health, and the finances of his company were in an even more delicate condition that they had been when Victor and I had made our record-breaking ten days and ten nights run. Running a racing stable then, as now, was enormously expensive, and it seemed as if AC, like many other motor firms, might have to give up racing altogether.

I was bitterly disappointed. I'd become attached to that little car which I'd driven for thousands of miles in the worst conditions. Still, I'd no intention of giving up because of a stumble at the first fence. I began wracking my brains to find another car which would go fast enough, long enough; over breakfast one morning the answer popped into my head – the 4½-litre Bentley!

The fact that I was switching from a David-sized car to a Goliath caused me no concern. Without finishing my breakfast, I telephoned the Bentley Company and made an appointment with W. O. Bentley himself, a man who had made a tremendous contribution to Britain's international motor racing reputation. He readily agreed to see me.

The following morning I arrived at the Bentley works to find not only W.O. waiting for me, but Captain Woolf Barnato, the diamond millionaire who backed the Bentley racing stable financially. Briskly I told them that I wanted to borrow one of their cars, why I wanted it, and where I was going to take it.

W.O. came to the point just as quickly. He said, 'We've only one car available – Tim Birkin's mount. He's driving it in several international races this year and Earl Howe is to drive it in the twenty-four hour race at Le Mans next month.'

His meaning was clear: if he lent me the car and I damaged it, Earl Howe and Tim Birkin, to say nothing of W.O. himself, would be displeased. However, I seized on his words to strengthen my argument. I said, 'That twenty-four hour run at Montlhéry will run it in beautifully for them. I hope to average at least a hundred miles an hour, which means I'll need a car that can be hotted up to do about a hundred and seven.'

W.O. said, 'Who's your co-driver?'

I told him, 'I've no co-driver. I'm going alone.'

Captain Barnato shot a glance at W.O. I saw that he was not very happy about that idea. For a moment there was silence and I knew that my fate was hanging by a very slender thread.

Then W.O. said to Barnato, 'I believe she might do it.'

I felt like cheering. I knew then I was going to get the car. Before they could change their minds I said, 'Do you think your engineers can squeeze a hundred and seven miles an hour out of her?' W.O. seemed a little dubious, but he told me, 'We'll see what we can do with the help of a high speed gear axle and three carburettors.' It all boiled down to the fact that I now had a car capable of taking the record.

When the mechanical details had been settled, W.O. posed another problem. He said, 'I'm afraid you've very little time to prepare, not much more than a week and maybe less. I hope that you won't blow the engine up, but after twenty-four hours running at that speed it may need a bit of attention. We've got to get it to Le Mans on time and in top condition.'

I recalled that Thomas Gillett had taken six months to prepare for his attempt on the record. He had trained for it like a boxer, and even had a masseur to pummel his muscles into shape because driving in those days took strength as well as skill.

Because he knew he was going to have a severe buffetting from the bumps on the track he had had a special leather jacket tailored for him with heavily padded areas and back; yet in spite of all these preparations and precautions he had been lifted out of the car after his record run.

There was no time to brood over such sombre facts. I said to W.O., 'I'll return your car, safe and sound, by June the seventh. I'll be grateful if you can let me have the services of a Bentley engineer and mechanics, and naturally I shall pay for their work; and I'll look after the transport charges, getting the car to Montlhéry, too.'

I had not thought seriously at that time about how much the enterprise was going to cost. As usual, funds were low and Aunt Maud's legacy would bear no more squeezing. W.O., however, came to my aid immediately. He told me, 'Don't worry about shipping the car or paying the mechanics. We'll take care of that. The Bentley will be waiting for you at Montlhéry. Good luck to you.'

I thanked them both and dashed home to telephone the French Automobile Club. I asked its officials to book the track for me and arrange for time-keepers to be present. They agreed to do so.

The following morning I contacted them again. They told me that the track was now booked for 6 June and 7 June, though they added with what sounded like genuine regret that the price had gone up somewhat since last I had been there. To hire the track for twenty-four hours would cost £134, compared with £250 for ten days and ten nights eighteen months earlier. Nevertheless, I arranged for the money to be sent off immediately, checking carefully this time that it went to the right people. I had no wish to have barricades flung up in front of the Bentley.

It was only then that I sat down to work out the cost of the enterprise in detail. By the time I had covered several sheets of paper with figures I realised that despite the generosity of W.O. Bentley I would need the help of at least one sponsor if I was going to break even. So I reached for the phone again, and made an appointment to see Sir George Beharrell, Chairman of the Dunlop Tyre Company.

Full of confidence, I told him that W. O. Bentley was lending me not only the car, but an engineer and mechanics. I had booked the track already, and naturally I was going to use Dunlop tyres. As soon as I broke the record, that important fact might at least be worth international advertising.

He listened carefully. Then he said, 'Little lady, you can't do it without a co-driver. Don't try.'

'I can do it,' I insisted. 'I will do it!'

Smiling, he shook his head and said, 'I still think you'd be ill-advised to try; but if you do and if you succeed, come and see me.'

To most people those words would have struck a note of cautious pessimism. To me, however, they had only one meaning: I was going to get sponsorship from Dunlop as soon as I broke the record; and by that stage I felt sure that I would break it. Leaving his office thoroughly cheerful, I went to Bond Street and bought myself a pale blue leather jacket for the occasion. It had no special padding, but I thought it looked very smart.

Throughout my racing career I never wore any special kit. I was never keen on overalls or slacks, but always drove in a blouse, tailored skirt and a string of pearls, except once when I added Madame Patrice's fireside fur rug to my driving wardrobe during the colder spells on the ten days and ten nights run.

Madame Patrice was the next person I contacted, booking a room at Château Montlhéry for the night after my record attempt. By 5 June I was on my way to Paris, alone this time because Victor had flu. I spent the night at the Hotel Astra.

The Bentley with the chief engineer and mechanics were at Montlhéry and I knew that they would be hard at work on the car giving it a final tuning. I knew, too, that they would not be exactly overjoyed to have a driver standing over them at a time like that; so instead of going out to the track I stayed in the hotel and wrote to my mother: 'Dear Mama . . . I'm over in Paris just about to make an attempt on the twenty-four hour record. I hope to drive the whole time myself and cover about two thousand miles in the twenty-four hours. If you buy Friday and Saturday's *Daily Sketch*, you'll be able to read about it. Expect to be back in England on Sunday. Will come and see you first opportunity. Love to you all. . . .'

The following morning I was up and out early. I hailed a taxi and said, 'Montlhéry, s'il vous plait. L'autodrome.'

In almost a whisper the taxi driver said, 'Montlhéry? *L'autodrome?*'

'Montlhéry,' I repeated, a little puzzled by his expression of awe.

'And quickly, please. Vite, très vite.'

He whipped off his beret, fumbled in the dashboard pocket and pulled out a white flying helmet. He put it on and had buttoned it under his chin even before I'd settled in the back seat. Then he gripped the wheel, hurled in the clutch and set off for the track as if he, instead of I, was trying to break records. He certainly knew the way and he certainly knew how to drive; but as he hung low over the wheel and tore round a mass of corners through the suburbs, I was flung from one side of the cab to the other.

All Paris taximen are competitive drivers to their backbones. All love sport – especially motor racing – and that man was determined to show me he was king of the road. Montlhéry was fifteen miles, but in what seemed like as many minutes he reached the track, skidding to a stop. Half-dazed I got out, paid him well over the odds and said weakly, 'Merci . . . Très bien . . . Magnifique!' At that he tried to hand me back the money, saying that it had been a joy to drive me. I managed to persuade him at last that his hair-raising brilliance deserved a reward. With that he bowed to me, climbed back into his cab and drove off sedately, his head held high and still wearing his white flying helmet. I have made many adventurous journeys on land, sea and air, but that taxi trip to Montlhéry on that June morning I shall always remember.

By that time it was 9.30 in the morning. The weather was dull and seemed a little ominous. I saw that the hurricane lamps were already in position round the perimeter and the sight of them not only brought back memories, but cheered me up. I had made my last record bid at Montlhéry in the middle of winter when night was longer than day. The lamps had been lit in the late afternoon and were kept burning well into the morning. This time it was June and the summer nights were short. I would need those lamps only for a few hours.

In the pits I met for the first time Wallace Hassen, Bentley's chief engineer, and two of his mechanics, Wally Saunders and Jack Sopp. A dreary drizzle had begun to fall and they were frowning at the sky. They said nothing about it then, but I sensed that they were unhappy about the weather conditions. A few months earlier there had been a bad accident at Montlhéry when a driver had skidded off the track while attempting another record and had gone straight through the safety barriers. But that was one of the hazards, of course, and I knew that a greasy track was not going to make the run any safer.

Together Wallace Hassen and I went through the driving schedule. I was to start at noon and pull into the pits every three hours for no longer than three minutes. In that time they had to fill the tank with their quick-filling taps and huge funnel, top up with water and check tyres and water. Wallace said, 'If we can make the pit stops two-and-a-half minutes, all the better.' I nodded.

Nobody mentioned how *I* would be refuelled during the run, but that was of small importance to me. As Madame Patrice knew well, I seldom ate when I was on a record-breaking drive. The exhilaration, the thrill of it, seemed to give me all the nourishment I needed. There was chocolate in the dash-board pocket of the Bentley, if I needed it, but I rarely reached for it. Moving would change the pressure of my foot on the accelerator for a second or two that that would change the rev rate. If the record was going to be broken, those revs had to be kept not only high, but consistent. Otherwise the engine mightn't stand the strain.

As the morning wore on the rain began to fall even more heavily. The steep banking had become so slippery that nobody could even walk up it. Thinking of the magnificent machine which was due in Le Mans a few days later, Wallace Hassen said, 'It's getting very greasy. Maybe you shouldn't make the attempt today. Maybe it'll have cleared by tomorrow.'

It was a sensible enough idea. In other circumstances I might have agreed; but perhaps it might rain for several days, and the car was needed for Le Mans. I said to Wallace, 'Don't worry. Last time I was here I drove on black ice. I'll have a practice lap and see what it feels like.'

Before there could be any further debate I got into the Bentley. It was vast compared with the AC . . . so vast that my feet wouldn't reach the pedals and my head barely topped the dash board. Wally Saunders went to the time-keepers' hut, came out with three cushions, and handed them to me. I put two behind my back and sat on one, which brought me close enough to the pedals and raised me high enough to see where I was going. The hand brake was a huge lever outside the car. I said to Mr Hassen, 'I don't expect I'll need that – but if I do, I'll have to stand up to reach it!'

28 In the four-and-a-half litre Bentley used for the twenty-four-hour drive at Montlhéry

Then I started my trial run. I reached 105 m.p.h. quickly, faster than I'd ever driven before; and I soon learned the difference between an AC sports car and a four-and-a-half litre Bentley. The extra speed meant I was much higher than I'd ever been on the banking, just a foot from the top. The old wall-of-death feeling I'd known before came back and with it the dizziness. I reckoned, however, that others had lapped just as fast and just as high. So it was simply a matter of sticking it out until I got used to it.

The bumps that had hit me so hard in the AC were even worse in the bigger, faster Bentley. At over 100 m.p.h. they became quite ferocious, particularly the brute that had overturned Victor. They pounded me, battering my shoulders, restricting my breathing. The mechanics had screwed the shock absorbers down as tight as they'd go to stop me bounding over the top, and this made the effect of the bumps even worse.

At the end of the lap I went to the control hut where three time-keepers from the Automobile Club of France were preparing their books to record my time on every lap. The chief time-keeper had been on duty during my earlier drive at Montlhéry in 1927. He greeted me with a smile and without any asides to his colleagues. There were no suggestions that they would be on their way home soon, that I wouldn't last long on my record attempt. They didn't even ask me if I had a spare driver. Instead they told me that they, themselves, had ordered spares. Three relief time-keepers, they said, were on their way from Paris, which showed that they thought I might complete the twenty-four hour drive.

I signed on and went back to the car. It was only half past eleven, so I still had plenty of time. Jack Sopp suggested a cup of tea and I said it would be very welcome. I needed some stimulants after my drive to the track in that taxi.

Then it was a minute to noon. By that time the rain was pouring down. I got into the Bentley, waved, and on the stroke of the hour set off on the first of over 1,500 laps.

I was so near the top of the banking, the car had to be held very firmly. Constantly it seemed poised to leap over the top of the track, especially at night when I had to drive by feel. I knew that I could not afford to lose concentration for even a split second.

After a few laps I settled down to a steady 107 m.p.h. the Bentley's top speed, faster than I had ever driven before or was to drive again until I went to Thruxton race track forty-five years later and touched 110 m.p.h. in the Ford Ghia Capri. Every fifty-seven seconds for the next three hours I flashed past the pits, keeping a close eye on my revs. Engines did not rev so high in those days and there could be trouble if I did not keep them at a constant 3,000. If I had gone at 3,500 revs for half a lap and then dropped to 2,500 there was a chance of damaging the bearings. That meant that not only had I to keep an eye on the rev counter, but take the weather into consideration, too. Downwind I had to give the car slightly less acceleration. Going upwind it needed slightly more to keep the rev needle on

29 I look on as the Bentley mechanics refuel the car with 'quick filler' cans

that magic figure of 3,000.

The worst part of that first three-hour stretch, however, was the effect of the bumps. Every time it hit one, the Bentley, shock absorbers screwed right down, shuddered and so did my body. My chest suffered most, making breathing very difficult. When I pulled into the pits for the first time, Wallace Hassen was standing by with a stop-watch to time the mechanics. Wally Saunders and Jack Sopp ran beside the car, unscrewing the fuel tanks before I'd even stopped. I said to Mr Hassen, 'Slacken off the shock absorbers!'

'I daren't,' he said. 'You'd go over the top.'

'Better that than suffocate,' I told him. So they slackened them. In under three minutes I was off again.

For the next twenty hours the routine never varied, except, perhaps, by a second or two. I became like an automaton, sitting rigidly, scarcely moving, with only two main thoughts in my mind: the rev counter and staying awake. The slightest shift of my foot on the accelerator affected the speed, but with concentration the average lap speed seldom varied by more than a fifth of a second. Every three hours I stopped for fuel, and for water and tyre checks. It was a relief to get out of the car, if only for a couple of minutes. Then back and off, a robot again for another three hours.

By that time night had closed in. My world shrank to the confines of the Bentley. The red storm lanterns were stars to guide me. I was averaging 105 m.p.h. and the car was going like a dream. If it kept going like that, I knew the record was mine because already I was ahead of schedule. Then, just before the dawn, one of the greatest enemies very nearly beat me: sleep. I'd fought it lap after lap that night, and then I must have drifted off. It was the change in the sound of the engine that woke me. I heard the rushing sound of the hoardings at the top of the banking; then I pulled the Bentley clear. We plunged down the banking and as I approached the pits I saw them flagging me in with a red lantern.

I must have nodded off to sleep for a fraction of a second. Any longer would have been too long . . . too late for me to pull away from the hoarding. Instead I would have shot over the top. When I drew in, Wallace Hassen told me I'd actually touched the hoarding. Someone said something about the suspension, but I wasn't listening. I got out and hurried to the pit for a drink of water to revive myself. I picked up a bottle marked 'mineral water', took a gulp . . . and felt as if I'd been struck by lightning. It was BP petrol, set aside for a spirit lamp. I choked and fought for breath. Somebody thumped me on the back and I managed to bring most of what I'd swallowed up again. That probably saved me and my record. My throat was still on fire, however, and it was fifteen minutes before the chief engineer let me back in the car – fifteen precious minutes which dragged my average speed down sadly.

I sat there, fuming, but at last was back on the track again, chasing those lost minutes. I cut out my last pit stop and drove continuously for six hours. That gave me two-and-a-half spare minutes. The higher the sun rose the nearer I came to the record. I knew it was within my grasp by that time, despite lost time.

When the sun was reaching its height I saw a flurry of activity in the pits. After one more lap they held up a huge board with the magic number *10* on it. It was a beautiful sight. I had just ten laps to go. They counted me down backwards like the space launches of today, just as they had done on my last Montlhéry outing. Then up went the figure *1*, the final lap. Just fifty-seven seconds later I drew up at the pits. Before I was even out of the car Wally Saunders and Jack Sopp were checking the engine. Mechanics are usually men of few words, but that time they seemed really excited about the car's performance and they even seemed quite pleased with me, too!

I walked to the time-keeper's hut, where they told me that I had covered 2,164 miles in twenty-four hours at an average speed of 89.57 miles per hour. I'd broken the record and the bumps had nearly broken my back. I was still tasting the petrol for weeks afterwards, but that gained me another sponsor. The BP Company didn't charge me for the fuel, not even what I'd swallowed. They simply advertised that their petrol had kept not only the Bentley going, but the driver too!

As I came out of the time-keepers' hut I heard my name called. I turned and saw Earl Howe, President of the British Racing Drivers' Club and the man who was to drive my Bentley at Le Mans, walking briskly towards me. He congratulated me and said, 'I thought you'd do it. In fact I came down early from Paris this morning to watch your last few laps. Would you be too tired to drive with me to Paris and have some lunch?'

'I'm never tired,' I said cheerfully, but I was exaggerating a little. Off we went to a beautiful restaurant in the heart of the city for a truly superb meal to celebrate. When coffee was served Earl Howe said to me, 'I'm proposing you for Honorary Life Membership of the British Racing Drivers' Club.'

Unfortunately I never heard him. I'd dozed off for a moment, just as I'd done when I nearly went over the top of the banking. For all I knew he could have been telling me I'd been banned from driving for life. His proposal, anyway, was accepted by the committee. Honorary Life Membership of the BRDC was and is a great honour. It has been conferred on fewer than a hundred and twenty drivers from all over the world since the Club was formed in 1928.

That night I went to Château Montlhéry for a good night's sleep before going home. Madame Patrice was waiting for me in the hallway. She threw her arms around me, kissed me on both cheeks and said, 'You did it!'

I nodded. Madame beamed and disappeared into the kitchen to prepare her famous scrambled egg and cheese supper. I ate it, went to bed, and slept for forty-eight hours.

Back in London I called on Sir George Beharrell. He shook hands with me warmly and said, 'Well done! My secretary has a little envelope for you.' When we had finished talking about the record-breaking drive, I left, not forgetting to collect the little envelope. In the street I opened it. Inside was a cheque for £1,000 . . . what I have called ever since 'manna from heaven'.

In the meantime the car had been examined thoroughly by Wallace Hassen and a team of Bentley experts. They announced that it was in perfect condition, and off it went to Le Mans for the famous 24-hour race. Soon afterwards I got a telegram from Captain Barnato, inviting me to Le Mans as guest of the company to do a lap of honour with him before the race because he had won the year before. Over I went, and this time I sat as a passenger while Captain Barnato drove me round the circuit.

Naturally I stayed on to watch the race, because I had a very personal interest in it. I sat there tensely, dreading that the engine which I had promised to run-in would collapse. In fact it behaved beautifully, though sadly it did not finish. It developed magneto trouble, which could not be attributed in any way to its twenty-four hours' marathon at Montlhéry, and was forced to retire after seven laps.

The Bentley Company, however, did well at Le Mans that year. Woolf Barnato and Tim Birkin won in a Bentley Speed Six. Three 4½-litre Bentleys, similar to that which I had driven, finished in second, third and fourth places. Later that year Tim Birkin took my record-breaking car to Ireland and won with it there.

Altogether those were hectic weeks even by the standards which I had set myself. Before they were over the Bentley Company organised a dinner in my honour.

The twenty-four hour single-handed record I set at Montlhéry on 7 June 1929, has yet to be broken.

Seven

Beating the *Berengaria*

MY SUCCESS encouraged me to tackle new records: when passing through Hendon, north of London, I had stopped to watch the speedboats racing on the Welsh Harp at Edgware, and my imagination was captured by the possibility of setting a record on water. I decided to buy an outboard. Such a speedboat is usually about twelve feet in length, and gets its name from the engine being attached to the outside of the stern by two large bolts. (These bolts have to be screwed down very tightly, or the engine may shift, and could part company with the boat: I was nearly to experience that.)

I called my new boat *Mosquito*. She was able to do forty knots with a special Elto Quad engine.

The motor boat club at the Welsh Harp organised races, placing a number of buoys on the lake, round which the competitors had to turn. Turning at forty knots in an outboard is a very tricky business, as the slightest mistake in handling can tip it over. So I did not win my first race; I was a learner, and not keen on being tipped into the water. It was not many days, however, before I was taking the corners full out.

I learned my lesson in my fourth race. On the second turn *Mosquito* took charge, tipped over, and threw me out into the cold waters of the Welsh Harp. From forty knots, I hit the water quite hard; my lifebelt saved me from cracking my ribs. It was after about fifteen races that I had the idea. Why not cross the English Channel in the *Mosquito* and create a record for the fastest time?

Nobody had tried this before, and once I had the idea, there was little which would stop me making the attempt. I soon arranged for *Mosquito* to be sent by rail to Dover, and when I arrived there, she was moored in the harbour. I tried out the craft there, and it was not still like the Welsh Harp. I realised that I would have to wait for a very calm sea. My patience had to last over a week, but then on 15 September, there was no wind, and the sea was calm as a mill pond.

30 Starting on the Channel crossing in the outboard

Now there was not a moment to lose; I knew how quickly the wind might change. The company who had sold me *Mosquito* was keen to help my attempt at record-setting, and had sent a large speedboat with a navigator to escort me to Calais. There I was to fill up with petrol and oil before making the return journey. Within twenty minutes I was off, the speedboat leading the way. I was clearly faster than the company expected, for I soon left my escort behind. By half-way across the Channel there was no sign of it, and the sun then had to be my guide. (It was pointless fitting a compass in the boat because of the excessive vibration.) Fortunately, I needed to go little further before seeing Cap Gris Nez in the distance. From there, navigation to Calais was easy, but the pounding and thumping over the waves, on top of the shaking, made the journey no sheer pleasure, and you can imagine my delight and relief when I reached Calais harbour and slowed up by the quay.

It had been arranged that a timekeeper from the Automobile Association would record my time of arrival, and as I rounded the buoy in the harbour, I saw him, watch in hand. I hailed him: 'Vive La France!', and then in a mad moment, turned for home. I knew that if I stopped the engine, I might not be able to start it again. (These outboard motors are started by pulling a string. They run on a mixture of petrol and oil, and indeed the plugs do often oil up.) Only now did I consider: I could only hope that there would be enough petrol for the return. I had in mind a record speed for the *double* journey.

Conditions were not so good on the journey back; the sun was disappearing behind the rising mist. I knew it would be possible to miss land altogether. Then suddenly out of the mist appeared the *Canterbury*, a cross-Channel steamer of which I knew the Purser: I had crossed a number of times on that ship with my racing cars on the way to Montlhéry, and he had always taken a great interest in my record attempts.

At forty knots, *Mosquito* was almost flying, and the bows were right out of the water. I passed the *Canterbury*, which managed only fifteen knots, as though it was standing still. I went close to wave to the passengers; indeed so close that I nearly tipped myself over in the process. I heard later that the Captain had sent a message to the Harbour Master at Dover: 'Something called *Mosquito* has just passed us and appears to be more or less flying; with luck it should be with you in about twenty minutes.'

He was right to say 'with luck', because the wind had now increased and little white horses speckled the surface. To make matters worse, my thumping over each wave-crest had started the engine bolts working loose, and the excessive vibration had compounded the problem. The jolts were terrific, and what with trying to tighten the bolts with one hand and hold on to the steering with the other, I was scarcely having an easy time.

My luck – and the bolts – held just long enough, and I saw through the mist the indescribably welcome sight of the white cliffs of Dover. The thought of 'home' gave me the extra determination I needed, and seemingly in moments, I shot up right onto the beach at Dover. I was so dazed that I forgot I was back. I started talking French, thinking I was still in Calais. All my concentration had been needed for my own problems. I had forgotten my escort speedboat; I now asked what had happened to it. Nobody seemed to know. In the exhilaration of success, I actually suggested that I should go to look for it in *Mosquito*, but fortunately someone pointed out that my steering was coming adrift, and that the rivets were coming through the floorboards.

An hour later I heard what had happened to my watchdogs: the engine had failed, when the sparking plugs oiled up, and I was in fact to watch the boat *towed* into Dover harbour.

Just as I was about to leave for my hotel (would you believe it!) the Customs officials came down to the quay to ask if I had anything to declare!

The double journey had taken 1 hr 47 min, the fastest any outboard boat had been across the Channel and back. The Company who built *Mosquito* presented me with a new boat; and indeed mine had sustained considerable damage. Later I put up a silver cup for anyone who could break my record in an outboard. Seventeen adventurous motor-boat enthusiasts like myself set off from Dover. The result of their attempts justified my tedious wait for a calm sea. They did not have the patience; and *none* of them reached Calais. Quite a number were picked up by the Royal Navy floating about off the Hook of Holland. Eventually I was asked by the British Motor Boat Club to offer the cup for some other record, one which would not be so troublesome to the Navy.

My first adventure in a speedboat had been a success: I was keen to continue my record challenging. The practical problems of finance were eased, since after the Channel crossing I received a bonus from the petrol company who supplied the fuel for this venture. The petrol companies were always very generous providing I agreed that they could advertise that their brand of fuel had been used.

My next exploit was not intended to be so dangerous as the Channel crossing. I decided that as I held the land speed record

31 Checking in at the time-keepers launch, before my attempt on the twenty-four-hour power boat record

driving solo for 24 hours, I would try to break the record for the longest distance ever covered on the water in 24 hours. The Cunard Company told me that the *Berengaria*, which held the Blue Riband for the Atlantic, had covered 691 nautical miles in 24 hours. For this 24-hour record the track was not Montlhéry, but the Solent, the backer not W. O. Bentley, but Scott Payne, famous in the power boat world, whose power boat company were the designers of Sir Henry Segrave's *Miss England*, the fastest single-engined boat in the world. Scott Payne provided two 23-foot power boats: two, in case one broke down.

A friend of mine lent me his large motor yacht for the time-keepers, as the record was to be officially timed. The course was to be around the yacht and a lightship, a distance of about six miles, and it was considered to be clear enough from the shipping lanes.

If the AC car looked small beside the Bentley, the *Mosquito* looked even smaller beside the power boat. I arranged to start at noon on a Friday, which rapidly proved the worst possible choice, because it was 'Mail Day', and liners were leaving the Southampton area every hour. At first their lights confused me.

I couldn't pick out the lightship, but at last I got used to it. I must have kept those lightship men awake all night roaring round them every six minutes or so.

The lack of variation meant that I began to feel like an automaton, going on and on. Every four hours I stopped at the yacht for refuelling, which took three minutes. From time to time I nibbled little pieces of chicken. (I'd told my friends I couldn't stand sandwiches because they reminded me of my motor racing record bids, with ham sandwiches from the glovebox always tasting of petrol. 'Give me anything,' I said, 'so long as there isn't bread on either side of it.')

It must be admitted that such driving was repetitive: by midnight I was beginning to get bored. The main trouble was staying awake, although at least if I did drop off for a moment I was *safe* enough, unlike the occasion in the Bentley.

Suddenly – catastrophe! The engine abruptly seized: there was nothing I could do to restart it. I sat in the silent power boat, helpless, drifting into the busy shipping lanes: all I could do was await help.

I could see lights coming towards me, big lights, and lots of them: it was a liner. Suddenly a searchlight from the yacht picked me up . . . then another from the liner. She was towering right over me, she seemed to be on top of me, there was nothing I could do . . . it was too late for her to stop, too late to veer. Even if she missed me her twin screws might suck me under; yet all I could do was watch with desperate hope.

Only yards away, the liner swept by. Her wash hit my craft like a storm. I shall not know how, without the help of the engine, I managed to ride that huge swell. But soon a boat from the yacht came alongside and towed me to safety. This record bid was evidently over. On arrival back at the yacht one of the timekeepers told me what I had just escaped from: the lights were those of the liner *Leviathan*. Everybody told me how lucky I was.

Scott Payne said tentatively: 'Mary . . . are you game to continue in the second boat?'

Already I had been at the wheel for twelve long tiring hours,

32 Myself and the boat before the start

but I knew the problems of bringing together the time-keepers and the mechanics. Scott Payne had provided *two* boats to meet just this eventuality. I answered:

'Well—— I'll have to, won't I? You did bring that second boat here in case the first broke down.'

Within ten minutes, my record bid re-commenced. The challenge drove me on against all tiredness: I had started, and I couldn't face the admittance of defeat whilst there remained yet a chance of achieving a record.

The twenty-four hours which followed do not stick particularly in my memory: the engine kept going on, and so did I. After those twenty-four hours going round and round the lightship, I pulled up alongside the yacht.

I waited for the chief time-keeper to bring me the news. I had completed 694 nautical miles, he told me. I had been at the wheel for 36 hours. I had broken the *Berengaria*'s record: it had all been worth it.

Eight

Flying Alone Around the World

MY BEATING of the *Berengaria*'s speed record was in October 1929, and as you will remember, I took part in the 1930 Monte Carlo Rally the following January. But by June 1930, I was wondering what to do with my remaining lives; there seemed no immediate possibilities.

I had an urgent appointment in London at one o'clock on a typically wintry summer day: I found myself walking down Burlington Gardens in London, with an hour to spare and nothing to do. Such things nearly always lead to my spending money – if I have any. On this occasion it led to much more, for what did I see in a shop window, but a full-sized aeroplane for sale. I had never seen one in a shop window before (and never have since, for that matter). I thought, 'What are we coming to now, when we can buy aeroplanes out of shop windows? Soon I shall be so old fashioned nobody will want to talk to me unless I learn to fly.' Immediately, however, I thought of my mother and how upset she would be if I turned up with an *aeroplane*; she had stood the worry of the motor-bike and the mad ponies; this would certainly be the end. 'No, flying is not for me.' I walked further down the street.

I came to another shop with a very pretty dress in the window: it was easily the best I had seen for years, and soon I was inside trying it on; the dress sealed my fate, for it didn't suit me, and I wandered back again towards the shop with the aeroplane, still with half an hour to spare before my appointment.

Perhaps the salesman had seen me looking in the window, for now there was a ticket on the aeroplane with the words 'Bluebird: Honeymoon model: ready to go anywhere'. I noticed the seats were side by side, and not one behind the other, as usually in light aeroplanes of that date. I was soon inside asking the price. I was greeted by a very smart salesman who said, 'Five hundred and fifty pounds, Madam,' and then added, 'chromium plating on the handles will be only five pounds extra. All nice and shiny for another five pounds.'

It all sounded so ordinary.

I said to him, 'Could you fly round the world in it?' 'Of course, Madam, easily; look, it folds.' Then he started to fold the wings back in the shop window. For one awful moment I thought he was going to say, 'Will you take it with you or shall I send it?' Telling him I would think about it, I hurried out of the shop late for my appointment. All the way back home to Esher I thought about the Bluebird. On arriving, there was a message from my husband to say he would be late for dinner. With those minutes to spare, I opened the atlas at a map of the world. It was then that the first idea came to me of what I would do if I bought the Bluebird.

I took a pencil and started to draw a line right round the world on the map, imagining I was flying over all the countries I wanted to see. I drew my line across the English Channel to France, then over France, Belgium, Germany and Austria, to Turkey, then across Turkey to Aleppo in Syria, over the Syrian desert to Baghdad, then along the Persian Gulf to India, across India to Calcutta and over the Bay of Bengal to Rangoon. Now, here was to be the parting of the ways: I couldn't make up my mind for a moment whether to fly to Australia. About that time an air race was being organised to Australia. I thought, 'If I go that way I shall be bound to bump into one of them.' I thought of the Kingston By-Pass on a Saturday afternoon: 'No, I want plenty of room in the air . . .' I took my line northwards over the jungles of Siam and French Indo-China to the China Coast, then up the coast to Hong Kong and Shanghai.

Now I came on the map to a little piece of water called the Yellow Sea; it looked so easy on the map, about an inch, and I drew my line across to Tokyo in Japan. (An inch on the atlas is about six hundred miles, but that dawned on me later.) Here I was faced with the Pacific Ocean if I wanted to fly round the world. The salesman had told me I would only be able to carry enough petrol for about seven hundred miles in the Bluebird, but remembering what he had said about the wings folding, I thought, 'That's what I'll do: fold the wings, put the Bluebird on a ship, sail across the Pacific and then open the wings again and fly on.'

So on went my line across the Pacific to Vancouver, then down the west coast of America over the great city of Seattle, to San Francisco and Los Angeles. From there I continued my line across the United States, over Arizona and Texas, till I came to the Mississippi River. Immediately I thought of my mother who was born near the banks of that great river, in a little town called New Albany in Indiana.

She used to tell me stories about the great gold rush in '49 and how my great grandmother had trekked across the plains of Texas and Arizona making the journey with my great grandfather in a covered wagon. More than half of the small party of pioneers who set out from New Albany were scalped by the Indians, and that when my grandmother was being born my great-grandmother was shooting through the cart wheel at them. I used to love these tales.

I drew a circle round New Albany on the map, with the idea in my mind that I would land there and find the house my mother was born in. Perhaps this might make her like the idea of flying.

Two days later I went to see my mother. 'Mama,' I said, 'I'm going to fly from Esher to New Albany.' My mother cried, 'You are going to do *what*?' 'Mama, try to understand, I'm going to fly, fly in an aeroplane. The salesman says it's easy, chromium plating is only five pounds extra; the wings fold, just think of that.' But she didn't; she was broken hearted, and I began to wonder how I would ever make her believe it was easy. I told her I would find the house she was born in, and after a while she began to cheer up.

Later she opened a drawer in her desk and took out an American flag, saying, 'Well, if you are determined to go, and

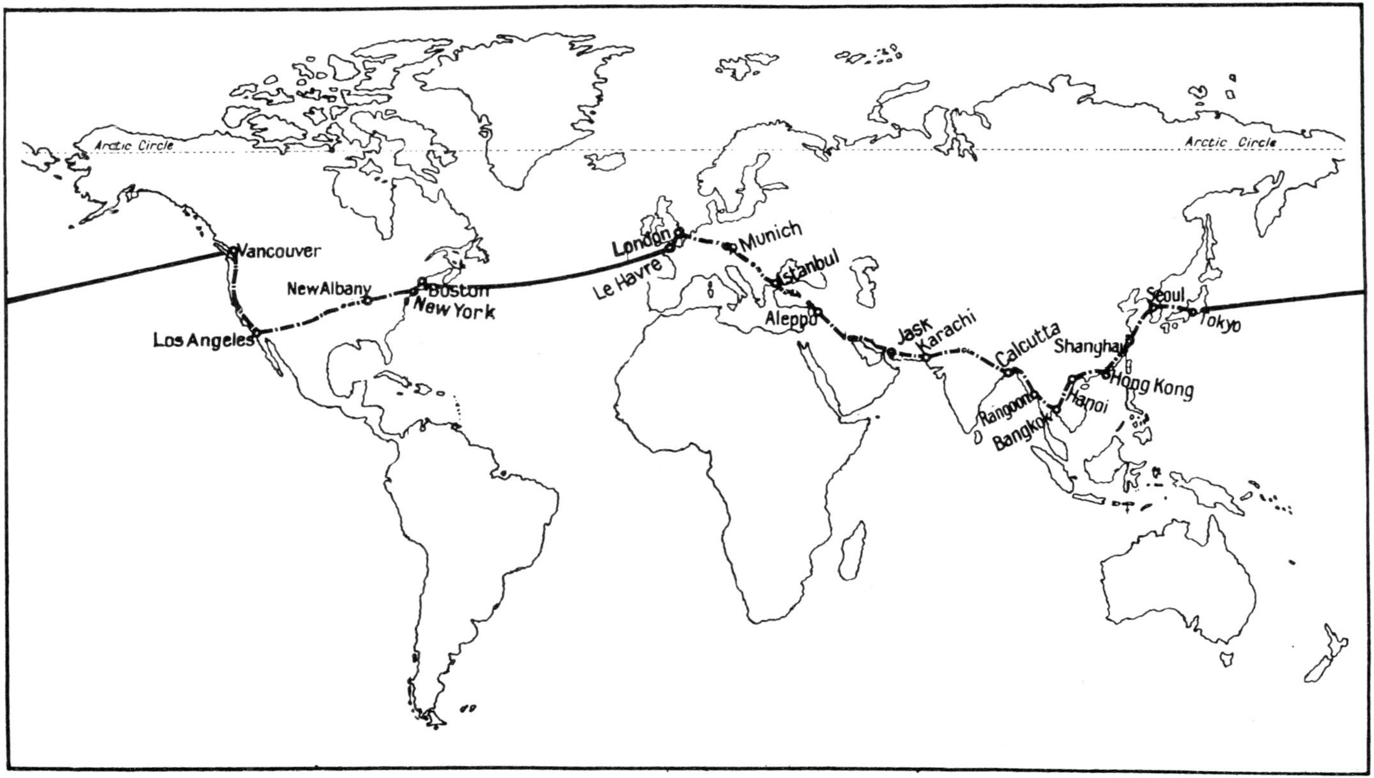

33 Map showing the Bluebird's flight

you really think that aeroplane is safe, and you find the house, drop this flag on it from the air, but, promise to take someone with you.'

'I can't, Mama, there will be no room in the 'Honeymoon model', for the spare seat will be used for a huge tank of petrol.'

Now my mother began to get miserable again, and I was at a loss to know how to convince her it was going to be all right. I reminded her about my nine lives. I also told her that everybody would be flying soon, but she said she would not be one of them. But before I left I do believe that she was fairly happy about my safety.

Two days later, to the delight of the salesman in Burlington Gardens, I bought the Bluebird. Coming out of the shop, I suddenly remembered something rather serious. It *was* rather serious. I had never been up in the air.

A few days later I called at the Air Ministry, only to be told that if I wanted to make the flight I would have to leave before the end of September because of the Monsoon rains in India and Burma. In those days we did not have blind-flying instruments, and it was therefore impossible to fly in the rainy season. The prospect of waiting another year and run the risk of my mother changing her mind about the safety of the flight made me decide that I would leave in September, and somehow learn to fly by then. Next, I called at Stanfords in the Strand to order the maps. They showed great interest in the map department when I asked for maps to be prepared for a flight round the world. The manager asked me when I had learnt to fly. When I told him that I had not been up in the air yet, but that I would learn to fly before I left, they asked me to pay for the maps in advance: £50. When I told my husband (a Scot) that I had paid for the maps in advance, he said, 'That's settled it; now you will jolly well have to go!'

Three weeks passed before I had time to arrange any flying lessons. On a flight like this there are so many things to organise: spares to carry, supplies of petrol to be laid down, and a hundred and one other things to think about. I sent the Bluebird to the Blackburn Aeroplane Company at Brough, where it was built, to have a fifty-gallon tank fitted in the spare seat. Two days later, I called myself to see the Chief Instructor at the aerodrome, to ask him if I could have lessons in flying.

'I'm afraid you can't,' was his reply. 'We have the Air Force training here. It will be impossible to give you a lesson for a fortnight.'

'That's no good,' I said, 'I shall be flying round the world in a fortnight.'

The pilot looked at me very hard. Then he led me to an office in the hangar and said, 'Wait outside for a moment.' I couldn't help hearing his conversation because he left the door open.

'A daft lass has arrived and says she wants to learn to fly because she's flying round the world in a fortnight.'

I didn't hear the rest because someone closed the door.

The pilot came out of the office.

'Mr Blackburn will see you in a few minutes.' Presently Norman Blackburn came out; he was smiling. 'So you want to fly, lass?'

'Oh yes, and quickly please,' I answered. 'I know what I'm doing. I'm used to taking risks, let me have the lessons.' How could he refuse? After all, I'd bought one of his Bluebirds.

'I'm only against you breaking your neck,' he went on. That day I had my first lesson in flying, and at the end of a week I went solo.

About that time I was questioned by the press, who asked me where I was going, but I didn't tell them in case I got lost. They started calling it a mystery flight, which just suited me, because I thought that then, wherever I landed they would think that that was where I was intending to go.

There still remained much to be done. I had to master the art of navigation, and so for days on end I pored over maps and charts, and tried to learn about the compass: it was all very difficult. Later a Master Mariner came down to Esher to teach me.

At dawn on 25 September 1930, eight weeks after receiving my pilot's licence, I was to leave Heston Aerodrome (now Heathrow Airport) on my great adventure. As I drove away with my husband from our cottage in Esher, my housekeeper, who had been in my family for twenty years, was crying: 'Oh, little lady, please come back!'

On the Aerodrome, my father was waiting. He looked very worried. The mechanics were working underneath the Bluebird. I heard one of them say, 'I don't think the —— thing will ever leave the ground.' They had good reason to say this: as someone remarked, I had indeed everything on it but the kitchen sink. There were so many things to carry; for instance, a spare propeller was vital, as other spares, and a special thing, a Dictaphone. You couldn't fly light aeroplanes with your hands off the controls in those days, and I wanted to keep a record of the flight. When Norman Blackburn noticed the Dictaphone being fitted, he said to the mechanics, 'She can't take that extra weight.' My husband immediately spoke up and said, 'Oh, yes, she can. Don't you stop her taking the Dictaphone, she'll never be happy unless she's talking.' So in order to lighten the load I threw out the parachute.

Someone handed me a telegram. It was from my Mother, with some final words of advice about the care of my health. The message ended 'the name of the house is "The Manse".' Until that moment my mother had refused to give me the name of her old house in America in the hope that this would discourage me from the flight. My father was then looking especially gloomy.

It was still dark, about four o'clock in the morning. There was a subdued murmur of talk among the mechanics, who were now fitting the spare propeller under the fuselage. For weeks past I'd lived in a whirl, talking of weight, loads, petrol capacity, weather conditions: it was unending. In spite of my warm clothing, I felt cold. Away in front of me, fingers of mist wreathed the trees in the half-light of the dawn.

No one had remembered to name the machine. I hurried away to the hangar to find a brush and some paint. These kept me busy for a few minutes as I painted the word 'Bluebird' across the fuselage. That finished, I sat down on a box of spares near the machine, and some friends came up and suggested some breakfast; but I wasn't hungry: I only wanted to be quiet and think. I was beginning to wish I'd never walked down Burlington Gardens.

Hello! A mechanic was shouting something, yes, they were ready.

34 'I painted the world "Bluebird" across the fuselage'

I climbed into the cockpit and fastened my straps; the mechanic called:

'Switch off, suck in.'

'Switch off,' I repeated.

The mechanic slowly pulled the propeller over to prime the engine, then,

'Contact.'

'Contact '

The engine spluttered into life and then settled, ticking over like a giant watch. Four minutes to warm up, then I opened the throttle, and the engine roared up to full revs.

'All set,' I called. The chocks were removed from the wheels, and in the dim haze I saw the little gathering of friends who had come down to bid me goodbye. I saw waving hands, and slowly raised hats, and was reminded somehow of a passing funeral. I started to taxi across the misty aerodrome, my husband walking beside me on the wet grass. I'd never flown a heavily loaded aeroplane before, nor had I been further than three miles from the aerodrome alone. I wondered, after what the mechanics had said, whether I'd clear the hangar and club house. My husband held the right wing as I turned into wind. A sudden pang caught me as I leaned over to say goodbye, then I opened the throttle. *Bluebird* trundled forward, then rose slowly.

'Don't be in a hurry to get her up,' had been my instructor's last words of warning. By the time I reached the club house I was fifty feet up. 'The worst is over!' I thought optimistically, as I climbed.

Making a circle of the aerodrome, and leaning out to wave at the little group below, I then struck out in the direction of Folkestone and the English Channel. The sun had now risen over the horizon, but navigation was difficult because of the early morning mist.

There was much to do for I had to find my way. I set a compass bearing and trusted to the forecast of the wind. Can you imagine my joy when about four hours later with a tail wind of 30 m.p.h. (the *Bluebird* could only fly at 75) I saw the words on the ground 'Munich Aerodrome'? I was to land there. I was so pleased to have reached my first goal, that I put a trunk call through to my husband to tell him the wonderful news. You know how one shouts at the other end of a telephone on a trunk call: I remember shouting:

'I'm here. I'm here.' But he didn't seem to hear. He kept answering, 'What part of Kent?'

That was the last time I heard his voice for many days, because I flew day after day from dawn to sunset. I was trying to break the record to India. All went well, and on the fourth day I found myself flying along the blue waters of the Persian

35 I circled over the control tower at Heston Aerodrome, (now London's Heathrow Airport).

Gulf. All that territory is some of the most desolate desert in the world. Temperatures are 120° in the shade. To come down anywhere there, I knew would be the worst thing that could happen to me.

It was three o'clock in the afternoon when I reached the Bay of Bandar Abbas, so I decided to take a short cut across the hundred and fifty miles of water, hoping to reach the landing ground at Jask before dark. It was a risk, I knew, because this part of the Persian Gulf is infested with sharks.

I'd barely got out of sight of land when I saw the needle on the oil pressure gauge drop to zero. Now you all know what that means on your motor car, but then you can pull up and stop. I suspected a burst oil pipe. I turned north, back towards the coast and said a silent prayer that the land would come before it was too late. How that engine ran for another quarter of an hour I just don't know; but it did, and in the distance I saw again the golden sands of the desert.

I glided down to land on what looked like the most lovely stretch of golden sand, delighting in my good fortune. I did not come gently to rest on the sand as I'd expected, however. The moment the wheels touched down, the machine shot forward at sixty miles an hour, tore through the sand, then buried its nose deep into it. I'd landed on a salt flat: dry on top, but mud underneath. I was thrown against the windscreen, hanging by my straps. The sound of tearing fabric and splintering wood was deafening as the propeller hit the ground. It seemed the end of the world to me.

Dazed, I released my harness and tumbled out on to the soft sand. *Bluebird*'s tail was sticking up in the air, and the engine was buried deep in the mud. My head hurt; there was blood trickling down my face. It was about four o'clock in the afternoon, the hottest time of the day, and I realised that I must take shelter somewhere out of the sun, for leaving the aircraft was like stepping out into a blazing furnace: flying at six thousand feet it had been quite cool. Still dazed, I sat down in the shadow of the *Bluebird* and waited for the sun to diminish. After about an hour, when it was cooler, I started to brush the mud away from the buried engine. At first a hopeless task, I became more encouraged as I proceeded. To my delight I found no damage, only the propeller broken, lying in pieces all over the place. The spare propeller was still safe, tied under the fuselage.

In my concentration, I did not hear them approach. I suddenly heard a strange noise, and looking up, found myself surrounded by the most extraordinary people I had ever seen.

They were Baluchis, the natives of that part of the Persian Gulf; they're half African and half Persian. I knew I must try to make friends with them quickly, so going up to the one that looked like their Chief – an old man with a big black beard – I shook him by the hand, and led him to the *Bluebird*.

I soon realised that the Baluchis were friendly, but needed a great deal of amusing, and I guessed that if they were not kept amused they would soon get tired of me, and possibly clear off altogether. I decided to show them my alarm clock, and wound it up, and put it on the sand. I don't think they had ever seen a clock before, and when the alarm went off, some of them ran away, to tiptoe back a little later. I was there three days before rescue came: I soon wished I'd never shown them the clock, for they made me wind it up every ten minutes.

The Baluchis saw what was necessary, and helped me to pull the *Bluebird* back into position. I hoped we could drag it on to a hard piece of sand, but it was hopeless, and the aircraft dug deeper into the mud. I knew it would be damaged if we tried to move it more. By the light of the moon I took off the broken stump of propeller, and after much difficulty, some of my tools having been left behind at the last landing ground, fitted the spare.

I wrote a message on a piece of paper: 'Please send help; have crashed. Bruce', gave it to one of the Baluchis and pointed in the direction of Jask. I thought then that Jask was about ten miles away, and learned only later that to get there it would be necessary to cross seven shark-infested creeks. When the man had not returned twenty-four hours later, I began to despair.

All the Baluchis left me at night, excepting the old man who stayed to guard me. I sat shivering after the heat of the day. I knew the desert was very cold at night but to experience it was another matter, and the wind blew the sand all over me. The old man was soon asleep under the aeroplane, but I kept awake listening to the waves breaking on the sand. I saw the dawn breaking and dreaded the sun as it rose in the heavens. 'Would the Baluchis bring me any water?' was my one thought. The terrific heat had made me desperately thirsty, and I had soon finished my small water supply.

About ten o'clock the old chieftain left me, and I was alone with the *Bluebird*. I wished the other Baluchis would come back. To my delight and relief, the chieftain returned a few hours later followed by two carrying a sheepskin full of water. It was brackish water, very nasty to drink, but it was water. Without it I had no hope of staying alive in the desert heat.

The next day came and about three o'clock in the afternoon I saw in the distance three warships sailing along the Persian Gulf, and remembered that Colonel Brisco had told me at Bushire (my last landing ground) that if I did not reach Jask he would send a warship to look for me. I had laughed at the time, but now it had happened. What hope had they of seeing me on that lonely stretch of desert? I guessed they were looking for me and the wreckage of the *Bluebird* in the sea. They disappeared over the distant horizon, not to return, and I was helpless to let them know where I was.

My hope of being rescued at all began to fade as I struggled back to the shelter of the *Bluebird.*

During the second evening the Baluchis began pointing towards the mountains. In the distance I saw horsemen coming across the desert. I had heard about the brigands who lived in the mountains, and how they would shoot strangers on sight.

The old chieftain seemed worried, and tried to push me into the cockpit of the *Bluebird* and cover me over with my rug. I tried to explain that this was silly, and instead walked across the desert towards the riders, taking my alarm clock with me.

On reaching the party I shook hands with the one who looked like the Chief Brigand. My alarm clock this time was a failure. No doubt they had seen heaps of clocks before. He was wearing row on row of bandoliers stuffed full of cartridges. His first word was 'Rupee', (they were perhaps Afridis from north-west India) so I led them back to the *Bluebird* and gave him all the money I had – about five pounds.

He seemed satisfied. He climbed into the machine and I handed him my flying helmet which he put on, and he amused himself working the controls up and down. I did not like one of his companions, an evil-looking man with bloodshot eyes, who seemed to follow my every movement.

Yet after a short while the Brigands prepared to go. The leader tried to lift me onto his horse, and I thought 'what a wonderful chance to get to Jask'. But my old Baluchi Chieftain caught hold of my arm, and pointed with his knife at his throat. I understood what he meant, and tried to explain to the chief brigand that I must stay with my machine. After they left, I felt yet more that I must get away from that place somehow.

On the second dawn, I woke the old chieftain and said, 'Take me to Jask.' But he only shook his head; I persisted, and packing up a few of my things (for example, my passport, I knew I must keep this), I wrote across the wings of the *Bluebird* the words 'I'm walking to Jask'.

And I started to walk across the desert. The old man knew I could never reach Jask, because to get there it would be necessary to swim across those seven shark infested creeks. He led me another way. I can't remember much about that walk; the heat was scarcely bearable. The sand seemed to be burning me up, and on two or three occasions I fell down and couldn't go on, but every time the old man pulled me up and shouted something in his strange language. I hazily remember collapsing in a daze under the shade of a lovely date palm. I'd reached the village where his tribe lived. Without his dogged persistance in driving me on, I would never have left that desert.

In the village I saw for the first time the Baluchi women. They were strange to look at, with long black garments, and rings through their noses. When they smiled (and they did smile), I noticed their teeth were painted black. They led me to a sort of mud hut, and disappearing, then returned with a great bowl of goats' milk. It was the first taste of anything nourishing I'd had during that three days. I fell suddenly and soundly asleep in the mud hut.

I was awakened by what seemed to be a war dance; all the Baluchis were dancing round the village and shouting and pointing to the sea. Getting up I saw coming towards me three men wearing white sun helmets. A lump rose in my throat, and I wanted to cry and laugh at the same time. Then an English voice hailed me across the desert.

'Hello, Mrs Bruce. Are you all right?', and as they reached me the leader of the party said, 'Cheer up, Mrs Bruce. We've brought you sausages for tea.'

Perhaps the calmness with which he treated my situation came from his familiarity with the desert regions. I discovered that he was Mr Murray, an officer of the Jask cable station of the Indo-European Telegraph Department and the local Police officer. But even then, desert rescue of lone aviators could not be a common feature of his duties.

He told me, after his party had carried me back to the shade of the date grove, what had happened. The Baluchi to whom I had given the message had struggled on regardless of all the hazards of the overland journey: he had swum the creeks, and marched on for two solid days, to collapse exhausted on the steps of the cable station. The rescue party had set out immediately by boat.

Mr Murray was concerned to return: 'This is hostile country; if we're found by brigands, we'll be shot on sight. We've come by boat to avoid the danger: we must move now.'

'But you must save *Bluebird*,' I pleaded. 'It's all ready to go, but I can't get it out of the mud.'

My persuasion was eventually enough: they arranged a kind of chair, and carried me the five miles back to *Bluebird*. (I had not realised that I had walked five miles through the desert.)

With the help of about twenty Baluchis and some ropes from the sailing boat tied onto the undercarriage, we started to tow the machine down to the water's edge.

I hoped that just above where the waves were breaking, the

sand would bear the aircraft and I could take off from there.

Mr Murray had brought a mechanic and a doctor, and two carrier pigeons. They sent the pigeons off with a message that I was found, and then the mechanic persuaded the engine to start, and climbed up and lay along the fuselage: he was going to travel with me in case there was any further trouble. He told me he'd done the same in the 1914 war.

The narrow strip by the water's edge proved just enough to let me take off: an hour later, I landed at Jask. It was three days since my crash landing.

Nine
On to Japan

I HAD been lucky to make even that short flight with the engine in the state it was after its ordeal in the sand. It needed a full overhaul before I could safely set out again, and the engineer had grave doubts that it would ever be truly airworthy again. The sand had worked its way into everything. But he started to repair the broken oil pipe, and to check the entire engine: after a week he was prepared to let me set off on my way to India.

I made a swift flight across that country to Calcutta, and then over the Bay of Bengal to Rangoon. Rangoon was where I had to make the final decision whether or not to go to Australia. It was there, on the map, that I hesitated when drawing my line. I took the northern route to Bangkok.

That city is the capital of Thailand, then Siam, and lies on the edge of the densest jungle in the world. The Siamese government tried to stop the flight. Their officials told me that there were fourteen hundred miles of practically uninhabited jungle to fly over in order to reach French Indo-China. There would be no petrol or weather reports, and if I came down in the jungle it would be impossible to search for me; but when they saw I was determined to go on they became quite helpful and the Commandant of the aerodrome said that if I could fly about five hundred miles, right in the heart of the jungle was a little village called Korat, a military camp. He said I might get petrol there, if I could manage to land on the parade ground.

At dawn the next day I was on my way, but all I saw that morning was trees, trees and endless trees, and now and again a sandy crocodile-infested river – the only thing which broke the monotony. If I missed this little village which was hidden in the trees, I wouldn't have enough petrol to return to Bangkok. My navigation depended on flying accurately by compass on the heading I had calculated. I was dependent on the wind not changing by too much, as if it did, my calculations, which allowed for the drift, would be futile. I had *some* room for error: from the height I was flying at, I could see about twenty miles to the horizon, and could pick out the larger features over all that radius. I believed that I could fairly readily see signs of habitation – changes in the colour of the forest, or a clearing, for example. Equally, I knew my speed and how long I had been airborne, so I knew when I should start to look for the features I expected.

But I must admit that I was lucky – very close to the predicted time, a darker patch of jungle caught my attention. I flew towards it, and eventually could see small, strange houses, built high-up on poles. I had at least found human habitation. Could it be Korat?

I flew over to see how feasible landing was. There was a clear sandy patch. That must be the parade ground! I decided to go down.

As soon as I'd landed, I was surrounded by Siamese soldiers. It *was* Korat. They smiled in welcome, and then almost immediately disappeared and brought two cans of petrol. I felt much cheered.

Then the soldiers turned *Bluebird* round, and faced it in the direction of Bangkok. I believe that those little soldiers flattered themselves that I'd come all that way on that lonely journey just to see them, because I shall always remember the look of surprise on their faces as I cried: 'Not Bangkok! Shanghai!' and disappeared in a cloud of dust.

I had now come to the worst part of the flight: for several hours, all I saw was trees again, and more endless trees, although I did disturb a herd of elephants, which stampeded. (The noise of the engine must have frightened them.) Climbing up high out of their hearing, I came shortly afterwards to a great river, the Mekong. This formed the frontier between Siam and French Indo-China, and borders the Annamitic range of mountains, now Viet-Cong country. At least the features here gave me something to base my navigation on! The mountains run right down from Mongolia, and form a barrier to all flying in that part of the world. No trail had ever been blazed that way by air.

About the same time as I actually reached the mountains, I saw angry black clouds coming up from the South, and with disconcerting rapidity, had been surrounded by monsoon rain. The days lost at Jask had cost me very dearly: I'd struck the break of the north-east monsoon in China. Within a few minutes I was flying blind: it was impossible to see ahead, and the rain appeared to be coming down into the cockpit in gallons, pressing me down onto the mountains. I tried to turn back towards the river, but could still see nothing but clouds. At least my heading told me that I was safe from the mountains.

One of the surprising facts of flying that one scarcely believes until one has experienced the effect oneself, is that it is quite easy to get disorientated in cloud to the extent that one can fly not level, or even inverted, without realising it. The movement of the aircraft can mislead one's sense of what is vertical. As I broke through the lowest layer of cloud, I found that I was indeed half upside-down.

Pulling myself out of my shallow dive, I looked at the river. I needed to get down soon, since I was running out of fuel, but all my strip map showed was jungle. (I was already short of fuel because I had been able to take on only a half fuel-load at Korat, as the aircraft had to be as light as possible to make sure I could clear the trees when taking off from that very short 'runway'.)

I decided that I would have to side-slip into the river before the engine stopped. I knew the aircraft would be damaged, but it was better to break it in the river rather than in trees.

Then the miracle happened: I saw beside the river a clearing. At some time previously, the trees had been cut down. There might be enough room to land, I thought, and in that situation, I was willing to take a risk. The *Bluebird* was soon bouncing and bumping over the rough ground. I came to rest in the middle of the clearing, the only damage being some fabric torn off the right wing, which had caught on some bamboo stumps. I was down, and that was all that mattered. I sat in the cockpit while the storm passed, and watched the majesty and grandeur of it all. I had never been in a tropical storm before. But beneath my wonder, I had a single thought: oh! how thankful to be down!

Then, as they do in the tropics, the storm suddenly stopped. The sky was blue again, but the sun was beginning to sink behind the trees. The thought of staying a night in that lonely jungle terrified me. I had to get out of that place, but with only half-an-hour's petrol left I knew of nowhere to go. Getting out of the cockpit and opening the locker, I looked for another map – a large-sized map – and found that if only I could have gone on up the river in another twenty minutes I would have come to two villages. One was called Lakhon on the Siamese side, the other Takhek on the French side. I tried to start up the engine but it was waterlogged. It was getting dark now. With a desperate effort on my part – oh! it was so hot – I managed to turn the engine over once more. It burst into life. I taxied right to the end of the clearing, then, opening up the throttle, tried to take off. But *Bluebird* would not climb quickly enough. Now you can't force an aeroplane to climb steeper than its climbing angle: if you try, you stall, you lose your flying speed; if you stall, that's one of the worst things that can happen, for you very easily go into a spin. So I kept the nose down to try to gather speed. I saw the trees rushing towards me, and as late as I dared, pulled her up. There was a crash. The undercarriage must have brushed the tips of the branches, but I managed to stay airborne. A few inches lower, and the aircraft, held back by its undercarriage, would have tipped forward and crashed into the trees. But I was flying up the river leaving the clearing behind. About twenty minutes later, by the light of the fortunately bright moon, I landed in a suitable field; where do you think it was? Immediately outside the house of the Siamese Governor of Lakhon. The large-scale map had saved me.

I was always lucky with governors. The Governor himself now came out to greet me. He spoke perfect English and agreed with me I was lucky to have escaped from the storm the previous day which was the result of a typhoon down the China coast. He asked me where I was going: I told him Hanoi. He was not encouraging:

'You will never get over these mountains. The peaks are twenty-five thousand feet high, and at this time of year we only have one day in twenty-nine that's not raining. You will do better', he continued, 'to take *Bluebird* to pieces and send it to China by canoe. It will arrive there in three months.'

Three months! I could cross the mountains in *Bluebird* in four hours. I told him I would rather wait for the one day in twenty-nine (but I didn't have to wait twenty-nine days. Only six.)

The Governor helped me fasten the machine down for the night, then escorted me to his house, where I rested for a while. He then took me along to a separate building, where he said I could live while waiting for the weather to improve.

So I was able to spend a while in Lakhon. The Governor took me around in his old 'Tin Lizzie'. It was a fascinating place: all kinds of strange things were on sale in the shops, from livestock to coconuts. The people seemed a very happy crowd, but that part of the country was rife with fever: I noticed so many of the children pitted with smallpox. The villagers lived in the strange-looking huts like those at Korat. These were built high up on poles, to keep them dry and out of the reach of tigers.

I asked the Governor if he could give me some petrol, and he said he could, but he only got fifty gallons once every three months, when the one and only boat came up the Mekong River. In the end he gave me thirty gallons, not really enough, but better than nothing.

About seven o'clock that first day I returned to my rest house. There was nothing to do so I went to bed, but I was soon disturbed by a sound of clanking metal. Looking out of the window I saw a number of Chinese prisoners stripped to the waists. Their legs were fastened together with chains. I'd heard that the worst type of Chinese criminals were sent to Siam and French Indo-China to make roads. There were no windows in

36 The mosaic temple at Lakhon

my room, and no shutters, there was no chance of worriless sleep. Once or twice by the light of the moon, I could see a yellow face peer in. I was very relieved when after a time they went away.

At dawn I dressed and went out to look at the river. The prisoners were near by, and one caught hold of the edge of my dress. But a Siamese boy appeared and shouted something, and they began to move off.

Two days later I went down with fever and a temperature of

104°F. I guessed it was malaria. The French Commissaire came across the river from Takhek to see me, and later sent a doctor. I felt too ill to get up the next day, but the little Siamese boy brought my meals regularly. By the third day I was much better, and I dressed and went across the river to see the Commissaire. He offered the hospitality of his comfortable house, but I told him I felt I should return to the Siamese rest house because they had been so good in trying to look after me. (But all the same, I wished I could have stayed in that comfortable house on the French side.)

Each day it rained and the mountains in the distance looked more terrifying than ever. So many things happened during those five days that it seemed almost a lifetime. The French Commissaire organised a tiger shoot, although I told him I didn't know how to shoot and wouldn't if I could – not a tiger. But he explained, 'We have to shoot the tigers here. They come into the village in the night and steal the children. Most of them are very hungry as they come from the mountains.'

So with his persuasion, I agreed to go, and the next day we went right up into the jungle where elephants were waiting. It was an intriguing experience, the gentle slow regular swaying of transport by elephant, made more so for me, since my particular animal kept taking me through the most prickly parts of the jungle. I had my camera and hoped to get a photograph of a tiger. Presently a shot rang out and some said, 'The governor's shot a tiger'. Within a few minutes we reached the spot and there stretched out on the ground was the tiger.

On the way back to the village we looked at the crocodiles in the river; ugly things they were. The Governor said some of them were three hundred years old; they looked it!

At the end of the fourth day I was getting weary of waiting for the weather to become good enough for my journey. It was tantalising, because in the distance between the storms I could see blue sky. It was difficult to believe that the weather was so bad a hundred miles away. By the fourth evening I was thoroughly depressed. Then on the fifth day, that was the Sunday, hearing there was a Roman Catholic Church on the other side of the River, and being a Roman Catholic myself, I went across by canoe to hear Mass and see the Priest. He was very concerned to know I was going to make another attempt to cross the mountains. He asked how long the journey would take; I told him, about four hours to reach Hanoi. He said, 'From the moment I hear your little plane cross my Church I will go on my knees and pray for you for four hours.' Then he gave me a St Christopher medal and told me to put it in *Bluebird*.

I eventually got over the mountains, but it must have been a miracle, because it was nothing to do with me that I ever reached Hanoi safely.

On the Monday, the sixth day, a telegram arrived to say that the weather was clear on the other side of the mountains, and that now was my chance to fly over the top of the clouds. But the Governor warned me: 'When you get over the top, don't try to come through the clouds because if you do you will probably still be over the mountains. Wait, and you will see the sea. The clouds will disappear on the other side.'

Promising to remember his advice about coming through the clouds I took off and started to climb up over the mountains, reaching nearly thirteen thousand feet, the highest the *Bluebird* could go. I was soon over the top of the mountains and the clouds, and it was one of the most wonderful, yet lonely feelings I've ever experienced. Nevertheless, I was happy because I knew that in two hours I should reach the China coast, and would be over the dreaded mountains. But two hours went by, three hours went by, four hours went by. Why didn't the sea come? Always in the distance I thought I could see the sea, but no, it was a mirage of the clouds, and before realising what had happened I looked at my watch and saw I had been flying for four-and-a-quarter hours. The needle on the petrol gauge had passed the danger mark and yet there was something about those clouds which made me think the mountains were underneath. Remembering what the Governor had said, I went on for another ten minutes.

Once when I was racing at Brooklands my husband had said, 'If ever you are going to hit anything it will be better to hit it hard.' We often say that when racing, because if you crash at a hundred miles an hour you very often get thrown clear of the wreckage, whereas at fifty miles an hour you usually get trapped in the car. This time I reckoned that if I was going to hit *mountains* it would be better to hit *them* hard, for there was no hope of even being rescued in those lonely peaks. Thinking it must be my end, I pushed the nose of the machine down and started to dive through eleven thousand feet of cloud. Every second I expected to crash as I hit the mountains, or worse still to come out over the sea knowing I hadn't enough petrol to get back to the land. For surely after over four hours I must be at least two hundred miles out over the sea. Then for the second time, a miracle happened. Instead of hitting the mountains or coming out over the sea, I saw beneath me the tall buildings of a town – the largest town I'd seen since Calcutta; then I saw a railway, and within a few minutes what looked like an aerodrome. I landed, and a crowd of people had soon gathered round to greet me. 'Where am I?' I said, and seemingly in one voice they answered, 'Hanoi. The capital of French Indo-China.'

I must explain what had happened: the wind had backed to the south whilst I was flying over those clouds. This had caused me to drift all the way over the mountains to the valley of Hanoi. If I'd come through even five minutes before I should have hit the peaks of the mountains, but I had come through at the right moment, and there I was safe and sound all among the Chinese.

At Hanoi I was welcomed by Colonel Premoral, Chief of the Air Staff. He arranged for *Bluebird* to be serviced, then drove me back to his home outside the town, where I met Madame Premoral. Her kindness and understanding of what I had been through over those dreadful mountains, helped greatly: the fever together with all my other difficulties had left me very low.

After even a brief rest of an hour or so, my spirits began to rise again. The general enthusiasm of the French people at the aerodrome helped give me courage to continue the flight as soon as possible. That night Madame Premoral had arranged a dinner in my honour and invited General Borzcki, the governor of Hanoi, to attend. I wanted to continue my flight the next day, but after persuasion from Colonel Premoral I agreed to rest one day. This would allow time for the mechanics to check carefully over *Bluebird.*

Crowds of French and Chinese people gathered round the aeroplane on the morning I left: many wrote their names on the wings. My hostess had driven me to the aerodrome, and I was about to say goodbye and climb into the plane when Colonel Premoral beckoned me forward. Then I recognised General Borzcki who had presided at the dinner the night before. Taking a beautiful gold medal from his pocket he stepped forward, kissed me on both cheeks and pinned the medal on my flying coat.

In French he told me that the Governor of French Indo-China had telegraphed that as I had made the first lone flight from England to Hanoi he wished to bestow upon me the Order of the Million Elephants and White Umbrella. Then in his best English he explained that this was a highly esteemed decoration, and told me the meaning of the order: it entitled me to call to my aid, if needed, a million elephants, and if I attended a feast I would be entitled to ride under a white umbrella.

All this provided no little encouragement, and it came at a time when I certainly needed it. Colonel Premoral had arranged for the Air Force band to be at the aerodrome, and as I climbed into the plane they played the French National Anthem. He had also arranged an escort of twelve Air Force planes. I was to have company for the first time during that lonely flight. I waved the pilots goodbye when I reached the Gulf of Tongking.

The Colonel had warned me not to make a landing on the coast because of bandits, who would most likely hold me for ransom. Two weeks previously they had taken two women missionaries, demanding money from the government, and because this was not immediately forthcoming they cut their fingers off and posted them to the French Consul to show what they would do. The money was soon actually on the way, but owing to road delay the bandits had shot them.

How thankful I was when I saw in the distance the island of Hong Kong. I thought it the most beautiful place I had ever seen, surrounded by its many small islands. I landed on the mainland at Kowloon, as there was no landing ground on the island. Sir William Peal, the Governor, had sent his equerry to meet me and take me to Government House where he and Lady Peal had invited me to stay.

The next day was Armistice Day, and after attending the Armistice service, I left for my next landing place, Amoy. There I was in trouble because I could not carry enough petrol for the next hop to Shanghai. I was welcomed and put up for the night by the manager of the Asiatic Petroleum Company. I remember how his wife tried to persuade me to have something to eat, but I had almost entirely lost my appetite after the previous few days, although I did manage to eat a scrambled egg.

37 Amoy harbour

I explained that I would have to land at Foochow for petrol. My host said, 'That is the worst place to land. There is always a war going on in that part of China. In fact,' he added with a smile, 'they fight every day of the week excepting Wednesdays, which is early closing.'

But my host was determined to do something. He arranged for an audience with Admiral Lin at his palace. (Although Chinese, he had been made an Admiral by the British Government because of the help he had given to our navy during the 1914 war.) The following day the British Resident escorted me to the palace, which was surrounded by a huge wall, with two iron dragons guarding the gates. We were challenged by a sentry, but when he saw the card signed by the Admiral, he led us at once to the palace. Soon Admiral Lin appeared, in British Naval uniform. He spoke perfect English, and asked how he could help me. I explained that I wished to land at Foochow for petrol. He smiled and said, 'I will send a telegram to my general commanding and he will arrange a more suitable place.'

As a result the Consul received the following telegram: 'Impossible for her to land at Foochow, but willing for her to land on my private golf course twenty miles north of the town. Removing the bunkers tonight'. So thanks to the Chinese Admiral I reached Shanghai safely.

I was greeted at Shanghai aerodrome by the Consul General, Mr Brenan, and driven back to the residency to meet Mrs Brenan. She was anxious for my safety regarding my proposed flight across the Yellow Sea to Japan. Mr Brenan was also very much against the flight as I would be right off the shipping route, and if a head wind blew up I might not have enough petrol to reach land. Eventually I agreed to follow the land route, which meant going two thousand miles out of my way; but then news came through that the landing ground at Tientsin was under water. So I decided to stick to my original plan and fly the five hundred miles across the Yellow Sea.

No sooner had I marked my course and arranged for a weather report, when a message came through from Tokyo explaining that the 'grand manouevres' were on, and that the

Japanese Emperor was attending them. There was a law in Japan that nobody may look down upon the Emperor. I was told by Mr Brenan that I would have to fly to Seoul, in Korea, and await instructions there.

That evening I was invited to visit H.M.S. *Bridgewater*, which was in Shanghai docks. The Captain arranged for one of his officers to swing my compass: that was a valuable service because I depended on keeping a correct course to reach Seoul with the petrol I could carry.

I was at the aerodrome before dawn the next day, and waited anxiously for the weather report. The Jesuit priests look after the Ziccawei observatory on the hill above Shanghai. They had stayed up all night so as to obtain all the information from various ships. The report was 'weather fair', and signed 'Best wishes, Father Glazie'. Someone brought me a little folding rubber boat – a kind thought – and it was put in the locker.

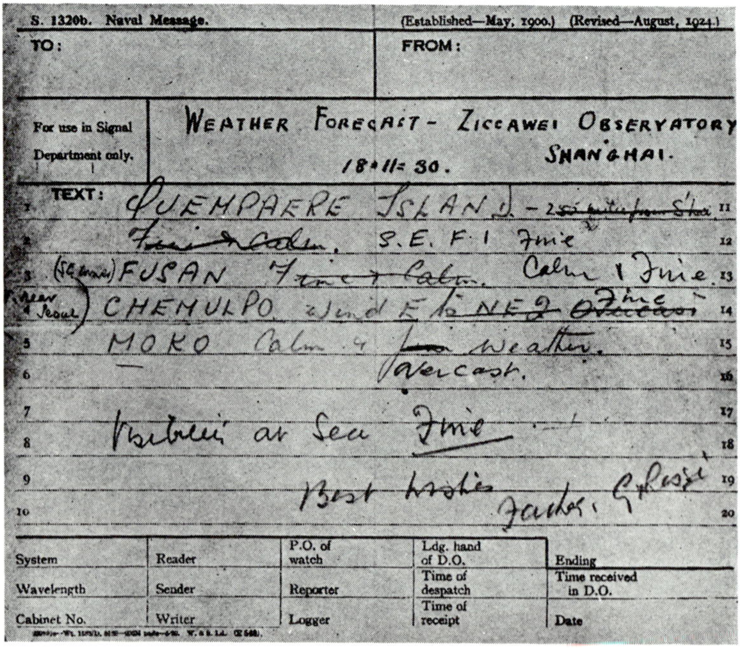
S. 1320b. Naval Message. (Established—May, 1900.) (Revised—August, 1924.)

TO: FROM:

For use in Signal Department only.

WEATHER FORECAST – ZICCAWEI OBSERVATORY SHANGHAI. 18-11-30.

TEXT:
1 QUELPAERT ISLAND – 11
2 S.E. F.1 Fine 12
3 FUSAN Calm & Fine. 13
4 (near Seoul) CHEMULPO Wind E to NE 2 Fine 14
5 MOKO Calm & weather. 15
6 overcast. 16
7 17
8 Visibility at Sea Fine 18
9 Best wishes 19
10 Father Glazie 20

System	Reader	P.O. of watch	Ldg. hand of D.O.	Ending
Wavelength	Sender	Reporter	Time of despatch	Time received in D.O.
Cabinet No.	Writer	Logger	Time of receipt	Date

38 The weather report

So now it was time to be off. There were a few concerned faces as I waved goodbye. The *Bluebird* climbed slowly with the heavy load of petrol. I noticed the *Empress of Japan* at anchor in the mouth of the Yangtse river: this was the ship I was to board in Yokohama in order to cross the Pacific Ocean as planned.

I dived down in the half light of the dawn and circled round, then looked back at what was to be my last sight of land for many hours. I felt lonely, but preferred the sea as a possible resting place to those dreadful mountains and jungle: I knew that if I came down in those I would never be found. It was after about five hours that I noticed a faint streak of smoke coming from the exhaust pipe. My heart sank. The note of the engine had changed. I switched off one magneto, then the other. All was well – only a small hole in the pipe, I guessed. The hours dragged; six hours passed, but no sight of land. I began to wonder: could I have missed the land? (It would be possible to pass over the Chosen (Korea) Strait and out into the Sea of Japan.)

The seventh hour passed and still there was no sight of land. The wind had dropped and it was raining slightly. I had to keep looking over the top of the windscreen, trying to find the land that did not appear. It was cold and I began to worry, but what use was worry on a flight like this? Then I saw in the distance what looked like a big cloud. But at last, this time, it was not a cloud – it was the mountains of Korea. What a joyous moment! Land at last, after all day over the Yellow Sea.

I flew in over numerous small islands; they were all mountainous and impossible landing grounds, but that did not worry me now, as I was glad to see any land at all.

Eventually, I reached Mokpo on the mainland, where there was a railway to guide me. I followed it through narrow passes between small and winding valleys in the mountainous terrain.

After about two hours flying over land, I came to a large valley, and could see in the distance a town I knew was Seoul. It was not difficult to find the aerodrome, which was large and beautifully laid out.

What a joyous culmination to the long flight over the sea it

39 At Seoul, I was greeted by children with flowers

was when I landed and was greeted by crowds of Koreans amongst which were two little children, who handed me a large bunch of flowers. The Consul and his wife, Mr and Mrs Oswald White, were there to greet me too, and drove me back to the Consulate.

Two days after landing in Seoul, I heard the Emperor of Japan was safely back in his palace, and I was now free to make the final flight to his country. A four-hour flight brought me to the Chosen Strait, and with a following wind I averaged 100 m.p.h. Just before reaching Hiroshima I saw in the distance a large number of aeroplanes carrying the Japanese flag. They came close – almost too close – to wave to me. The Japanese Government had sent them out to escort me to Tokyo.

Then came one of the greatest thrills of my flight: Fujiyama, the Holy Mountain, in the distance. I relaxed and admired the beauty of its snow-covered summit. How often that beautiful mountain appears on tapestries or in paintings!

And then came the magnificent reception at Tachikawa

40 I was escorted to Tokyo by Japanese aircraft

41 The welcome at Tachikawa aerodrome, Tokyo

42 At Tachikawa, with Miss Bouku,
one of Japan's pioneer aviators

aerodrome, Tokyo. The Japanese rushed round my plane when I landed, many giving me flowers. Their enthusiasm was such that the mounted police had difficulty in restraining them. When some degree of order had been re-established, I was welcomed by Japanese government officials, and the English Chargé d'Affaires who handed me two telegrams: one from the British Air Ministry and the other from Sir Alan Cobham. Then a member of the Japanese Government handed me a beautiful pearl necklace which had been sent down by Mr Mikimoto, Japan's famous culture-pearl king. One little girl handed me a painting of Fujiyama.

Amid cheers I was led through the crowd by General Nagaoka. He was known as the 'grandfather of aviation' in Japan.

(He had one of the longest moustaches in the world and would always hold it out for the photographers to take a picture!)

As we drove through the streets I noticed that many of the houses were decorated with British and American flags. No doubt it had become known that I was on my way to America to find my mother's home.

I was amazed and delighted by the number of people lining the streets, as we made our way to the Imperial Hotel. I was to stay there as the guest of Mr Kishomoto the steel magnate for a few days, before moving to the British Embassy. (The Imperial Hotel, a very large American building was earthquake-proof. During the great earthquake of 1923 it was almost the only building left standing, I was told. This proved to be reassuring information.)

After seemingly endless photos had been taken I managed to move towards my suite, but even on the way up the stairs, a photographer took a final flashlight photograph with a flash I thought must be from dynamite!

A number of firms and people were kind enough to offer help: after a short rest I came down into the hall to meet Mr Le May, Manager of the Rising Sun Petroleum Company, who had suggested that he take over my affairs and supply me with secretaries to deal with my correspondence.

My reaching Tokyo was celebrated by one long round of feasts, where generally I sat on the floor and ate with chopsticks. The most popular drink appeared to be green tea, with no milk or sugar. The Chairman of the Empire Aviation Society drove me to the quay in Yokohama to meet the Captain of the *Empress of Japan* which was lying at anchor in the harbour, having crossed the Yellow Sea. As I walked up the gangway a little Japanese girl gave me a battledore, a symbol of their national game.

I was to sail across the Pacific on the *Empress* on 4 December. Mr Le May had arranged for the *Bluebird* to have its wings folded and be towed behind a lorry to the quay. Everything now appeared to be going as the salesman had said in the shop in Burlington Gardens: 'The Bluebird can fly anywhere, easily'.

43 'My reaching Tokyo was celebrated by many feasts, where I sat on the floor and ate with chopsticks.'

Before I retired to my suite that night, Mr Le May warned me: 'Don't worry if the hotel shakes a bit during the night; we generally have a small tremor once or twice a week.'

I had not been asleep long when I was awakened and to my astonishment saw sparks coming from the electric radiator. My bed began to slide towards the window. The tremor soon became very violent, and the hotel rocked. Vases fell off the mantlepiece.

'This is a real earthquake', I thought aloud. I opened the door and saw Japanese people rushing down the corridor in ordered panic with bundles in their arms. To think I had flown all this way, encountering so many troubles, to be greeted by an earthquake! Then suddenly the tremor stopped and all was briefly quiet. Then a different noise ensued: fire engines were dashing through the streets.

I heard the bell-boy calling something in Japanese. He was assuring the frightened people that all was well. Mr Hamaguchi, the manager of the hotel, came to my suite to re-assure me that there was nothing more to worry about. Considering what had happened, everyone seemed remarkably unperturbed. Familiarity, perhaps. He took me the following day to the centre of Tokyo, where there is a monument dedicated to 'the Nameless Dead': in the earthquake of 1923, over ten thousand people fled to the Square in the hope of escaping the burning houses, but were trapped. Perhaps after events like that, one treats milder earthquakes without concern.

My particular earthquake, fortunately, erupted not under Tokyo, but further north in the mountains. But the English people who worked in Tokyo told me that it was difficult to relax with the continual possibility of tremors, and indeed, happy as I was amongst the Japanese, I found it hard to sleep peacefully after the experience of that night. I was happy to think that on 4 December, I was to sail to Canada.

Ten
Homes at Last

SO THE *Bluebird* and I sailed to Vancouver. How lovely it was to be able to forget for a time about the business of flying. I told my friends later that I had danced across the Pacific: I was quite truthful, because there was dancing in the ballroom of the beautiful ship every night. I had company too: Mr and Mrs Pratt made me feel at home. I had met them in Tokyo, where Mr Pratt was a director of the Standard Oil company. After all the excitement of Tokyo, I would have felt lonely without them. Further, Mr Pratt explained that he was arranging for one of the company's large aircraft to escort me over the mountains from Vancouver to San Francisco.

I enjoyed the voyage across the Pacific, especially the dancing every evening. On the third night it was announced that there was going to be a fancy dress ball on the second Monday. I said to the Purser: 'Surely we are not going to take two weeks to get to Vancouver?' He then explained about the Date Line which we had to cross. I should have remembered Jules Verne's book *Around the World in Eighty Days*, and how he thought he had lost his bet only to realise he had won by gaining an extra day when he crossed the Line.

So on the seventh day we all went on deck to have our first sight of Vancouver. Several large aeroplanes flew round the ship as we neared land: Mr Pratt had arranged a welcome.

At last we pulled up alongside the quay in Vancouver, and a few hours later the *Bluebird* was towed by lorry to the aerodrome. To my delight I was greeted by an old Irish friend, who put me up for the night. But I was in a hurry to leave for Seattle, as the weather, though cold, was sunny. I feared the fog, which made flying very dangerous with no blind flying instruments.

44 The *Stearman* escorted me to San Francisco

A very large aeroplane called the *Stearman* was on the aerodrome, ready to carry my luggage and escort me to San Francisco. The pilot, Captain Looff, appointed for this job by Mr Pratt, warned me that flying was not going to be easy after Seattle; there was a danger of ice forming on the plane. All American planes were fitted with de-icing equipment. Captain Looff explained that it would be possible to collect half a ton of ice on my machine in less than five minutes. In England nobody had much experience of this. Hoping for the best I left Vancouver on the 16 December for Seattle, followed by the *Stearman*.

It was during this journey that the Bluebird nearly caught fire. In the rush to ship the plane on the *Empress of Japan*, the mechanics in Yokohama had not noticed the small hole in the exhaust pipe. I could smell something burning and felt the rudder bar getting hot. I signalled to the *Stearman* by dipping my wings, that I was in trouble. Captain Looff led me immediately to an emergency landing ground in Victoria

Island. It was as I thought when crossing the Yellow Sea, a hole in the pipe; on inspection we found the flames were actually playing on the spare tank in the cockpit. Fortunately, a director of a nearby large factory came to my help, and plated over the hole. My usual luck seemed to be with me still.

This trouble over, I was soon on my way, and landed in the large town of Seattle. I had now reached the United States. During the voyage across the Pacific I had picked up quite a lot of American slang, so I felt quite at home: now was the chance to use it!

That night I was invited to a dinner by the Aeronautical Association of California. Their members told me that it would be very cold flying in an open cockpit in the dead of winter. In an unusually practical presentation, a member gave me a thick woollen jumper and a balaclava to put over my flying helmet. How right they were! I was nearly frozen later, crossing the Shasta mountains to San Francisco. Before I left, the Mayor of Seattle presented me with a large key and told me I had the Freedom of the City.

When I arrived at the aerodrome I noticed that still more names and messages to England had been written on the wings.

With the *Stearman* in my wake I climbed to ten thousand feet and could see in the distance the Cascade mountains. All too soon I ran into a sleet storm. Captain Looff's ominous prediction was all too true: I noticed a thin layer of ice forming on the wings. The *Bluebird* began losing height as the weight of ice increased, but I was nearly over Mount Hood, over 11,000 feet high. As I dropped to a lower altitude the ice began to melt slowly from the wings. I knew I was saved, and it was with a sigh of relief that I reached Sacramento Valley and the warm sunshine of California. I had, thank goodness, no longer any need to fly over high mountains.

The people of California were warm too: they showed their enthusiasm in many ways when I landed in San Francisco. The Chief of Police (it struck me how different he was to PC Parker), took me in his car to the Mark Hopkins Hotel. The police car was escorted by about fifteen police mounted on motor-cycles, their sirens blasting. How I enjoyed going so fast through the town, without a quarrel with a police constable as a consequence!

Later in the afternoon a member of the Aeronautical Association drove me to Mills College, where my mother had gone to school, and I was able to see her name in the school register.

I wished I could have spent more time in San Francisco, for I liked this city better than any I had seen except Hong Kong. But there was no time to dawdle; I had a long journey before me to reach my mother's house, and then New York.

On 12 January I flew on to Los Angeles. The landing ground there was easily the best I landed at. It was famed for its modern runways. I was greeted as usual by one of America's unflaggable Mayors – they often for their sins have to be present on these occasions. I was later escorted by a director of Warner Brothers, the film company, to visit the studios of Hollywood.

After that experience, some friends I knew in Los Angeles suggested that I go with them to the police headquarters, where there was an outdoor revolver range. The Chief of Police, one of the crack shots of America, gave a wonderful display; he shot two clay pigeons at once with two revolvers. As a special final display, he shot the ash from his sergeant's cigar. Then he said: 'Now, missie, I will shoot the ash from *your* cigarette.'

My excuse that I didn't smoke did not deter him. One of my friends persuaded me: 'Let him do it, dear – it will be another exciting experience for you.' My habitual love of risks decided me to take the risk. I walked about twenty yards to the end of the range, where the Chief lit the cigarette he had given me. I waited for him to shoot. There was a bang, but the ash was still on my cigarette. 'I'm dead' I thought. But then I heard his voice apologetically: 'Better luck next time'.

I was decidedly not keen on a 'next time', but someone handed me a cigarette holder and I used this for his second attempt. There was a bang, and a shower of ash in my right eye gave me the welcome tidings that I might yet continue my flight.

San Diego was my next stop. From there I started my long flight across Arizona and Texas, to New York, several thousand miles. Arizona brought back to my memory the stories my mother had told me about my great grandmother trekking across the plains in a covered wagon on that gold rush of '49. At Phoenix, I was given a letter from the Governor of Arizona for His Majesty the King in which he sent the greetings of the people of Arizona and said that it was the first time an English woman had flown alone across his country.

When I reached Texas, the head wind was so strong that I was only averaging about 40 m.p.h. I flew low over the railway line, past hundreds of oil wells. Soon I was overtaken by one of those fast American trains. I noticed waving handkerchiefs, and I felt sure the passengers were laughing at my slow speed. Only when the train stopped at a station did I pass it.

On reaching El Paso I had a magnificent view of the Rio Grande. By then I was once again at six thousand feet, and it was very cold. Following the ridge of the Apache Mountains, which now acted as a guide (the railway had disappeared into a tunnel), I began to feel tired and hungry, and was thankful when Pecos came into sight. Underneath me, out of that tunnel, that same train was back in view; it passed me this time as if I were standing still.

I stayed the night at Dallas. About two o'clock the next afternoon I saw from the air the wide waters of the Mississippi River. I thought of the evening at Esher when I had drawn the line round the world and planned to fly to my mother's home town. My dream was coming true.

By now I was receiving telegrams from New Albany each time I landed, telling me how preparations were being made for me to drop the American flag on my mother's old home. It was nearly dark when at last my goal came in sight. I flew low over the town, but had to land in Louisville, Kentucky, on the other side of the river. There was no landing ground in New Albany. Mayor McLinn welcomed me when I landed, and with a police motor-cycle escort, we crossed the bridge, to be greeted by crowds of people who had heard about the flag-dropping business.

45 New Albany from the air

The next day Mayor McLinn made a speech:

'Mrs Victor Bruce is to be our guest. The idea of coming to this city, the birthplace of her mother, prompted her dramatic and adventurous flight in a small plane from England over Europe, Asia and our continent. She will, in a short while, drop an American flag carried all the way from England on her mother's old home. We feel very near to England today with this ambassadress of goodwill and citizen through blood-ties in our midst.'

An hour later I dropped the flag, and it actually landed on the roof of the house. This flight was my farewell to New Albany and it was a happy ending to a wonderful day. My first 'home',

46 The Manse, my mother's house in New Albany

I had reached. My mother in England was delighted when she heard I'd dropped the flag.

And now for Baltimore, my last stop before New York. I was asked to land there on an airstrip outside a factory, instead of on the aerodrome. This was to be my undoing. I found the airstrip. I nearly nosed over on the muddy ground on landing; the take-off was to be disastrous.

I feared the *Bluebird* would not have enough power, limited to so short a take-off run, to clear the high-tension cables surrounding the strip: Knowing that I was expected to be on time in New York some two hundred miles away, I felt pressured to make the attempt. The *Bluebird* rose slowly, held back by the thick mud. I saw telegraph wires and cables uncomfortably near and tried to climb. I rapidly lost flying speed, stalled, and went into a spin, I hit the ground, and spun round several times. In one respect, my luck kept with me as usual: except for a cut on the head, I was unhurt. But I was broken hearted. To think that the plane was smashed so near the end of my flight! I just sat down and wanted to cry. But someone consoled me: 'Don't cry, dear. You have crashed outside the Glenn Martin Aeroplane factory, one of the largest in the world. They'll help.'

47 The result of trying to climb too fast

It was worth trying. I made my way to the factory office and asked if it was possible to speak to Mr Glenn Martin. I was immediately shown into his office, the windows of which overlooked the airstrip and the crashed plane. I said directly: 'Please, Mr Glenn Martin, can you get it mended?' He knew what had happened: he smiled and said he would do all he could. That night he put ten men to work on the *Bluebird*, and five days later it was an aeroplane once more. He did still more: he sent his tractors out to extend the airstrip. Everything is done quickly in America – perhaps that is the reason (being half American myself) that I am always in a hurry!

The next morning, I cleared the cables safely, thanks to Mr Glenn Martin's wonderful help; I found myself flying over the great skyscrapers of New York. I dived low along Broadway, then 'beat up' the Statue of Liberty: I had promised my mother I would have a good look at it. Then I flew round and round the Empire State Building, at that time the tallest skyscraper in the world. I noticed some waving hands from the top storey.

I landed on the Glenn Curtis aerodrome, where the police were waiting for me. I received a good telling off, but I got away with it.

48 The Glenn Curtis aerodrome

A member of the New York Flying Club took me to the offices on the top floor of the Empire State to chat with the young ladies who had waved. They said they had enjoyed seeing an aeroplane so close. (One said she had seen the colour of my eyes.)

My mother was delighted when she heard I had taken such a good look at everything.

Mr Pratt was in New York. He called at my hotel, to say that he was arranging for the *Bluebird* to be put on the French ship the *Ile de France*, which was sailing for France two days later. He told me to rest and not to worry about anything, but just enjoy the voyage. I certainly did; there was a real French atmosphere on that ship. I found the *Bluebird*, its wings folded, on the boat deck, all amongst the deck quoits. The passengers enjoyed writing their names on the wings. By then there were at least two thousand signatures on the fabric. Some even wrote on the propeller.

49 Lifting the *Bluebird* onto the *Ile de France*

I met some very interesting people on that voyage, amongst whom was Esnault Pelterie, the inventor of the joy stick. He told me that he was the second person to fly an aeroplane; he built his own plane and tested it out on the sands at Le Treport in France. He had needed to overcome many difficulties, chiefly those of the control system. He explained how he felt he needed a third hand. For a time he used two pieces of string to control the wing-warping (the precursor of aileron control), one to each wing. He held the strings in his mouth and had to lean over when he turned, to bring the wings into the right position. He decided that this string business would not do. He had to think of some other way of working the controls.

His eventual answer was the universal joystick control system, which to this day is used on all aeroplanes. The basic principle is precisely the same, although on *Concorde* it is electronically manipulated.

He was a very interesting man to meet, and he was then

50 Amy Johnson, myself
and Winifred Spooner at Croydon
Photo by courtesy of Sport and General Press Agency

designing a rocket car to go to the moon. I offered to be his first passenger.

The journey to France was completed in six days, and I felt very excited when I saw in the distance Le Havre harbour. We moored at the quay and a crane lifted the *Bluebird* on to a large lorry which was waiting to take it to the aerodrome.

The following day I took off for Croydon. Amy Johnson and Winifred Spooner flew to the English coast to escort me, which I very much appreciated.

The flight to Croydon was indeed short compared to some of those I had recently made. I was very soon gliding down to land. It seemed scarcely possibile that I was truly home again. Victor and my father were there to welcome me, and many of the friends who had seen me off from Heston that misty September morning had come there too.

My small son Anthony, led by his grandfather, soon reached the plane as I pulled up. Tony's first words were: 'Oh Mummie!

51 Mr Montague, Under-Secretary for Air, reading the address of welcome from the Air Ministry
Photo by courtesy of the Keystone Press Agency

You're an hour late.' I might as well have come from Brighton.

Then I was dazed with excitement as I listened to Mr Montague, the Under-Secretary for Air, reading an address of welcome from the Air Ministry.

I am often asked what happened to the *Bluebird*. She was going into a London museum, but the Blackburn Company (who gave me a new Bluebird) were anxious for the machine to go on show round the country. First she was put in the Underground station at Charing Cross (now Embankment). There were many messages on the plane as well as signatures. I was there one day with some friends, when an elderly lady found a message from her daughter in Vancouver. She was quite overcome; she told me she had not seen her daughter for twenty years since the latter left England as a young bride.

The plane stayed at the station for a month, watched over by police. It came to no harm. I wonder if an aeroplane might be put on show in an Underground station today?

Eleven

Air-to-Air Refuelling

IN 1932 I HEARD that aircraft in America were being refuelled in the air. I decided to give long-distance flying in Britain a new horizon. (No aircraft had ever been refuelled in the air in Britain and nobody there seemed to know of a safe way of making contact between two aeroplanes.) Hearing that there was a large flying boat for hire in Gibraltar, I consulted the builders of the boat, Saunders Roe, in Cowes. They told me it had three Gipsy De Havilland engines, and might be very suitable for my proposed endurance flight.

The flying boat had been used to carrying passengers across the water from Gibraltar to Tangier, some twenty miles. The service was a failure because of the rough seas, which caused constant cancellations. The problem was how to get the plane back to England. *I* could not do this because I had never flown a flying boat, or even anything so large.

Saunders Roe agreed for their test pilot Captain Scott, and a mechanic, to accompany me to Gibraltar, check over the plane, and fly us back. We were a little worried when we reached Gibraltar to find that the flying boat (which was called a Windhover) had been left out in the open, there being no hangar to put it in. The mechanic checked over the engines: they appeared to have come to no harm and started up quite easily. We soon took off from Gibraltar, reaching Alicante, in Spain, the same day. The next morning on take-off, the worst happened. Captain Scott was at the controls, when at about two hundred feet, all three engines cut out. The sight of the three dead propellers at that height could mean only one thing: we were going to crash. I saw a cottage and a woman and some chickens running. (One sees everything so vividly on such occasions.) It looked as though we were going to hit the cottage: Captain Scott just kept the Windhover on a straight downward course. Then about fifty feet from the ground he turned the plane, and missed the cottage by a few yards. We ploughed through an olive grove (leaving a piece of wing in a tree), then over a road and into a wall. There was a shower of bricks in my lap, but we were both down unhurt: a magnificient piece of flying by Captain Scott, although of course the plane was very badly damaged.

I soon got over the shock, and began to worry about the Windhover: however would we get it out of that olive grove and back to England? We did. The local people were splendid, and a lorry soon was hired and the wings and fuselage loaded, but two lorries proved necessary. Another one was amazingly speedily procured, and after only about three hours, all was ready for the long journey to Gibraltar. There, a telegram was waiting for us. It was from the director of the Bibby shipping line, and read: 'Put your plane on the next ship sailing for England; there will be no charge.'

People took a wonderful interest in pioneer flying during those early flying days. Help was always forthcoming.

So the Windhover eventually reached Saunders Roe in Cowes. It appeared that the carburettors had become slightly corroded, causing the engine failure. Within three weeks the firm had the plane repaired and ready to take to the air. An extra 100-gallon tank had been fitted in the fuselage, with a hand pump to send the petrol to the main tank. We needed this extra fuel to get us through the night, as it would not be possible to take on petrol in the dark.

Next I had to choose a crew. Certainly, two extra pilots were needed. The Royal Air Force gave special leave to Flight Lieutenant John Pugh and Flight Sergeant McLeary. John Pugh was a highly skilled pilot who had received the Air Force Cross for his flying in the meteorological flight at Duxford aerodrome, an RAF base. He used to fly up to twenty thousand feet every day, whatever the weather, in order to take the upper air temperatures, so that weather reports could be produced.

52 The Saunders Roe flying boat at Cowes. I am in position in the front hatch

I felt confident with him as a co-pilot, because I knew that, in the event of engine failure, he would get the plane down safely if it was at all humanly possible. I bought from the Air Ministry Disposal Board a Bristol Fighter, a fine aeroplane. It too was fitted with a 100-gallon tank in addition to its own petrol tank. The Bristol was to be our refuelling machine. Victor, T. Sparkes and J. Watson volunteered to act as refuelling crew.

Apart from taking part in flying the Windhover, I was chosen to crawl through a small hole to the hatch in front of the plane. Once in the hatch I was to grab the refuelling pipe. In order to keep the pipe steady, a butcher's weight was tied on the end. The first test was a complete failure. I managed to grab the pipe but was nearly hauled out of the hatch. Apart from this there was the danger that the pipe would foul one of the propellers.

We now knew that we would have to think of some other method of making the contact. I went home that night feeling very depressed. It had taken many months to organise the flight, only to be frustrated over this pipe.

53 Demonstrating on the water what I had to do in the air: reaching up for the cable

Then we had an idea: why not use an extra aeroplane? Join them with a length of one hundred feet of cord. Then arrange for the Bristol Fighter and the extra plane to fly at 1,000 feet on a given course, side by side with the cord stretched between them. The Windhover could then be flown towards the cord: I would catch it, and even if I missed it there would be no danger to the propellers. We tried this scheme out the following day, using a Gipsy Moth as the second plane. This method proved a complete success. I climbed into the hatch, caught the cord (I had tied some little red ribbons to it to make it easily visible) and then cut the cord releasing the extra plane. The contact was made! I now had a cord between me and the refuelling aircraft, and could haul in the fuel pipe. I fixed the cord to a winch just outside the hatch, and it was wound in to the rear of the fuselage, where McLeary was waiting. The refuelling plane now flew about fifty feet above the Windhover. McLeary soon had the petrol pipe; the nozzle was put into the tank, and within five minutes a hundred gallons was abroad.

54 Contact made: the refuelling plane is above

This method of making contact sounds very complicated, but it worked like clockwork. During the sixty-three hours we were in the air, the Windhover was refuelled eight times while circling the aerodrome. But all was not well. On our first attempt at Portsmouth, fog closed in as night approached. Then the lights in the plane fused; luckily the radio continued to work and we were able to keep in touch through a Marconi wireless van.

Just before the dawn, with the fog still covering most of the South of England, all three engines stopped. We had used up

55 The Marconi van for ground-to-air radio

more petrol than expected. There was not a moment to lose, as we were flying at only three thousand feet. I made my way in the dark to the pump which was to be used to start the petrol flowing from the extra tank. I wobbled the pump up and down. Suddenly the engines burst into life as quickly as they had stopped. We must have been very near the sea or ground when this happened.

By morning the fog cleared, and we were relieved to see the Bristol fighter take off from the aerodrome with our fuel. Down below the watching crowd laughed and cheered when John Pugh boomed over the radio: 'It's getting cold up here. Send down my pullover and two bottles of beer.' This was soon done with a rope attached to the refuelling cord. Knowing that we might get a lot of fog if we stayed over Portsmouth, we sent a radio message to the chief of the aerodrome at Ipswich asking if we could use his aerodrome as our base. We knew that on the East coast there would be less chance of fog. Permission was readily granted. All went according to plan. We continued to refuel regularly every eight hours for three days.

Then John noticed that the oil pressure had dropped to nought on the starboard engine. A cat walk had been fixed along the wings so that he could make any minor repairs to the engines. Switching off the faulty engine, he hitched himself to his safety belt and hauled his way out along the wing to the now silent engine. He worked on it for what seemed like an age, but the main oil pipe had broken, and he found it impossible to repair. He came back from the wing in despair, saying 'It's no good; we will have to come down.' I handed over the controls, and John made a perfect landing in the harbour.

We would naturally have liked to have stayed up longer. Our consolation was that we were the first to refuel an aircraft in flight in England, and had played a part in convincing many, including the Air Ministry, that there was a great future for air-to-air refuelling.

Twelve
Flying Circus

IN THE SPRING of 1933 I was invited to join a flying circus called British Hospital Air Pageants. Its aim was to tour Britain with sixteen pilots and a parachutist, putting on displays for charity and helping to make people air-minded by giving them joy-rides. The shows were to start in August.

Hospitals got seventy per cent of the takings and those who flew the planes or parachuted from them got thirty per cent – just enough to cover their own expenses. The leader was C.W.A. Scott, famous for his flight to Australia. Fliers, all of them well-known, were to provide their own aircraft.

I accepted the invitation and said I would supply two aeroplanes for the show.

A short while earlier I had bought a single-seater Miles Satyr, one of the smallest aircraft in the world. It was the personal plane belonging to F.G. Miles, owner of the Miles Aircraft Company at Reading. I arranged with John Pugh, who had helped me with the endurance flight, to do aerobatics in the Satyr. Then, as the organisers were anxious for me to have a plane which would give the passengers a thrill, I called at Coley's Yard in Chiswick, a well-known graveyard for obsolete RAF machines. Many of these aeroplanes were in quite good shape, but because they had been replaced by the RAF with something faster, they were sold for scrap. I arrived at the yard just in time to save a fine Fairey Fox bomber from being sawn in half.

'Stop!' I cried to the man with an electric saw in his hand. 'This plane is going to fly again.' Then I bought it for £2 10s., and its Rolls Royce Kestrel engine for £10.

I had the precious machine loaded on a lorry and sent to

56 Myself and the Miles Satyr

Hanworth aerodrome for overhaul: it had to meet the requirements of the Air Inspection Department.

Before I could fly passengers for hire and reward I had to have a 'B' licence. I commenced study at once. I asked the same Master Mariner who helped me before with navigation when I was preparing for my round-the-world flight if he would instruct me. He was pleased to help, but it was nearly three months before he decided I was ready to take the examination. I received my 'B' licence a month before the start of the Pageant.

The team included Pauline Gower, who flew a Spartan bi-plane, similar to a Moth, and Dorothy Spicer who serviced it. She was the only woman in the world to hold a mechanic's A, B, C, and D aeronautical licence. Pauline and Dorothy must have taken up over a thousand passengers during the show. They charged five shillings for a straight and level flight, which attracted quite a number of people.

John Pugh always put up a fine performance with his aerobatic flying, on the Satyr. He used to fly upside down, slow roll, and spin. (Spinning in the Satyr was not a very nice sensation because it would easily go into a flat spin, difficult to get out of.

That's where the expression 'going into a flat spin' comes from.)

Another very interesting part of the show was Captain Brie on the Autogiro, similar to the helicopter of today. He used to give a very good display, landing vertically beside the wireless van.

We flew from town to town, never knowing what kind of landing ground we would find. Sometimes the fields were so small that we wondered how we would get into them, and even more how we would ever get out of them.

The Fairey Fox was a very powerful aircraft and could touch 200 m.p.h. in level flight and a good deal more in a dive. It was three times the size of the Bluebird, and landed very fast. I needed instruction for two weeks before I got used to the speed, and landing in small fields. I had only flown the Bluebird until then; that was a slow-landing machine.

The organiser of the show was McEwen King – not a flyer, although he did select the landing fields in which we were to land! He asked me if I could think up a really thrilling flight to attract passengers. My answer was a dive at about 250 m.p.h. I would then pull out at about fifty feet from the ground and then fly low over the crowd. This stunt rarely failed to attract a queue, and I think I thoroughly enjoyed doing it. My passengers had no fear; they wanted not only to loop the loop, but fly upside down, and everything else the plane could do. The pilots in the show called my special flight the 'Death Dive'. Officially it was known as the 'Fox Dive'.

Bombers in those days were quite small, not the vast machines they are today. The Fox had only two seats, one for the pilot, and one for the man who carried the bombs. I was able to squeeze two not very big passengers into the rear seat. I charged them 15s. each for a five minute flight. Colonel Fitz-Maurice (who flew the Atlantic in 1936) was our commentator. He used to announce over the loudspeaker: 'Roll up for the "Fox Dive" have the thrill of your life for only fifteen shillings.'

One day when operating at Reading a very nice builder booked for the 'Fox Dive'. He had paid extra for a very special high-speed dive. This time I pulled out twenty feet above the wireless van. He appeared very pleased with the flight. As he was leaving he took hold of my hand. I thought he was saying goodbye (and wondered why he had not done this *before* the flight). As he left and let go of my hand he said, 'Buy yourself something Miss'. Opening my hand I found a shilling. I am sure my man would have been hurt if I had given him his shilling back.

There was really only one passenger who gave me real trouble. He was a very fat man, and he took up so much room in the cockpit that I was unable to squeeze the second passenger in. I therefore charged him five shillings more for his flight. He wasn't very keen on paying extra, so I gave him a specially long flight, to make up for it. I'd just started to adjust the tail plane for landing when I heard a tearing noise. I realised that he had got his mackintosh tangled up with the control apparatus. We were in trouble! Without the tail plane in the correct position, it was practically impossible to land. Every time I tried to wind, he shouted 'You're ruining my mac!' It was no good shouting back that he'd better get his mac out of the apparatus or we'd both be killed, because he wasn't in a co-operative mood.

So I decided to try and land with the control jammed. Twice, my speed was too fast – it was like trying to land nowadays without the flaps out. My fellow-fliers on the ground knew something was wrong, but the crowd, of course, had no idea. The fire brigade and ambulance were alerted. On my third attempt to get down, I succeeded, although I ended up with my propeller just touching the hedge of the boundary. (We'd no brakes in those days.)

I was relieved that we were both in one piece, but my passenger was simply furious. He didn't even notice the fire brigade and ambulance standing by; he was only worried about his mac. He demanded his money back for the flight and £2 damages for mac repairs on top of it!

The only manoeuvre I didn't like was looping the loop. Captain Phillips usually did that. He was a wonderful pilot, admired for his pluck by everyone in the show. He was the only pilot I had ever seen take off and go into a loop, at about one hundred feet, coming out certainly not more than fifty feet from the ground. This was the most thrilling flight in the Pageant.

Once, when he was not available, I was asked to do it. When my passenger was in the cockpit, I did everything in my power to get him to change his mind. I suggest racing the express train from Reading to Paddington. 'It's very exciting', I told him. We can fly alongside it only a few feet from the ground and wave to the passengers.' But he was adamant; 'I've paid to loop the loop and I'm going to loop the loop.' So loop the loop we eventually did.

Another popular turn in the circus was known as 'Catch the Bandits'. Three of our pilots would drive a car round the landing ground, while John Pugh would chase them in the Satyr, diving down close to their car. Then two of our team would tear across the landing ground and arrest them. This little act (with Colonel FitzMaurice making it exciting over the loudspeaker) always pleased the crowd.

The end of the display was generally the parachute drop, and most onlookers waited for this. The parachutist usually managed to arrive on the landing ground, although this was not always easy, especially if there was a strong wind.

Life with the circus was packed with incident, and for a while dogged by bad luck. Once, for instance, I had a five shilling bet with John Pugh that I could land the Satyr on the green outside Stafford in a shorter distance than he could in the Fox. I spotted the green with a large crowd waiting. It was bordered on two sides by small houses and just in front were telegraph poles, carrying a bank of about a hundred telephone wires. When you're flying, you do not see the wires, just the poles; one has to remember they are there. Unfortunately I forgot: the poles were hidden behind houses.

Thinking of my bet, I approached the green as slowly as I dared. Suddenly there was an almighty crash. I thought I had hit one of the houses, because the noise was terrific. Then I realised that I had flown into the telephone wires. The Satyr and I must have remained hanging in the wires for at least half a minute. Then the wires gave way and we fell fifteen feet to the ground with a bang. But I had won my bet. I was exactly four yards beyond the fence which bordered the green. I tumbled out of the plane with telegraph wires all round my neck. John Pugh said he did not think it worth while trying to beat me for five shillings. Except for a big bump on the head I wasn't hurt, but I was rushed off to the doctor who told me that I had slight concussion.

There was quite a crowd gathered to watch that exhibition. I heard one old prophet of doom mutter, 'Don't worry, this is only the beginning of it'. How right he was: an hour later C. Evans (the parachutist) landed on the chimney of one of the houses I had missed; he had to be rescued by the fire brigade.

The Satyr, of course, was badly damaged (and it was not insured). On top of the repair bill I got another from the telephone company: £80 for 80 broken wires.

As I felt sure the newspapers would be full of all this by the evening, I thought I had better telephone Victor to tell him I was all right. There was an unusual delay, so I asked to speak to the Supervisor. I told her I had an urgent message and must get through quickly. She replied: 'I'm sorry, but some silly fool has flown into the telegraph wires, and we haven't a line to London, let alone Esher.'

While the Satyr was being repaired I hired a Gipsy Moth to take its place in the show – and that led to more trouble. In those days aircraft were still started by mechanics swinging the propeller. They had no brakes, and chocks were jammed under their wheels to stop them running away. One day our mechanic swung the propeller of the Gipsy Moth while it had no pilot aboard and no chocks to hold it back. The engine started. The Moth began buzzing round the field in circles, then it picked the Fairey Fox as its prey, crashed into it, and put it out of action until the end of the month.

The Fairey Fox featured in another incident. John Pugh was flying it when it caught fire in the air. He had to stand up in the cockpit to avoid the flames, which were all around him. He managed to get it down, by side-slipping to the ground into a corn field, where the machine turned over on its back. John put up a courageous show, pulling out the two women passengers from the burning plane just before the petrol tank exploded.

While this was going on, Colonel FitzMaurice was still announcing on the loudspeaker: 'Two more for the Fox Dive, two more for the Fox Dive. Have the thrill of your life. Dive from two thousand feet. The thrill of your life.' Someone whispered to him: 'The Fairey Fox is down in flames.' Without a pause and without changing tone, he announced: 'Two more for the autogyro, two more for the autogyro – two more for the safety plane.' I was reminded of my mother's favourite phrase in the midst of a catastrophe: 'The show must go on'.

I was unable to find another Fairey Fox: I left the show.

In most ways, of course, flying is more reliable today and safer, but we had one advantage in the thirties: we landed slowly, and had a sporting chance of climbing out of a wreckage unhurt. I had got so used to turning upside down that I was surprised if a whole year went by without a mishap. I wasn't always the pilot. I often climbed out of the wreckage when I was the passenger.

The circus achieved both its objectives. It raised a good deal of money for hospitals, and it certainly helped to make those who rolled up to watch more air-minded.

A month later I decided to organise a flying display of my own. A local estate agent found a suitable field beside the Kingston By-pass, at Hook.

John Tranham the famous parachutist had offered to make a night drop, the first time this had ever been attempted.

The show started with a garden party and several of my flying friends offered to give five-shilling flights. My special flight was over Hampton Court. My passengers loved this flight as they were able to see the Maze.

It had taken several weeks to arrange the night descent. The Major of the local Searchlight Brigade agreed to send his men and the searchlights. Loudspeakers were fixed in two trees so that our commentator could tell a short story, to the effect that an enemy spy was about to land by parachute.

The display was a terrific success. Hundreds of people made their way to the landing ground. One of my friends took John Tranham to about four thousand feet in his Moth. Then John jumped with the searchlights shining on him.

He landed in a large elm tree at the end of the field where two of my flying volunteers dressed as soldiers were waiting to arrest him. The commentator made all this very exciting and also amusing. It was an added entertainment for the crowds, for it proved necessary to call the fire engine out; John was stuck in the tree until a ladder was produced.

I decided not to put this display on again as there was too much risk to the parachutist, if he landed at night.

It was shortly afterwards that I saw an advertisement which diverted my attention, and was to launch me on a new career. It was in the *Aeroplane*, and it read: 'Aircraft required to carry newspapers to Paris.'

Thirteen
Croydon Days

I KNEW that Air France had been carrying newspapers to Paris for some years, but had recently lost one of their newspaper planes in a fatal crash at Croydon. I gathered that the company was anxious to be free of the contract. I called on Air France's traffic Manager, who said that he hoped I got the contract, for he would then be able to sleep more peacefully at night. I was to understand his feelings: I can truthfully say I never really was at peace during the years I ran that service. One of the main dangers was early morning fog. Weather reports were unreliable in the very early morning, and instrument flying was in its infancy.

The distributors of the newspapers were pleased to give me the contract. I formed a company, and called it 'Air Dispatch'. The service became known as the 'Dawn Express'.

We set up headquarters at Croydon Aerodrome, and bought two De Havilland Dragon twin-engined biplanes, which cruised at 100 m.p.h. We then engaged two former RAF pilots and two wireless operators. No matter how bad the weather the newspapers had to get to Paris on time. Our motto was that of the old Pony Express: 'The Mail must go through.' We delivered the papers to Le Bourget aerodrome before seven in the morning, and they were on the breakfast tables of Paris by eight; it was the first time this had ever been done. Soon our contract was doubled. Such a service provided a wide range of incident. One day half-way across the channel an engine failed with the heavily laden plane at 4,000 feet. It began to sink slowly. Snowy, the wireless operator, began ditching the cargo. Out went the *Daily Mail*, then *The Times*; next the *Daily Herald*. Gradually the Dragon began to lift. The *Daily Express* was the

SPECIAL RATE SERVICE AT ORDINARY RATE CHARGES

Freight, whether of a fragile nature, ordinary merchandise, machinery parts, or livestock can all be sent by air. The less time taken in conveying merchandise and freight of all kinds means less risk of damage together with minimum cost of insurance. Quick delivery means service "par excellence." You keep ahead of competition by being up to the minute with your transport problem. Markets are often lost by reason of delay through traffic congestion. To have your goods for sale for only two hours before others means a decided increase in your turnover.

The key to this Express Transport Service is in your telephone or a letter to us stating your exact requirements, such as the nature of the consignment, weight, destination, etc. We will advise you how to pack same, and the formalities that have to be attended to.

Collection vans operate in the London area for the collection of parcels at your convenience. Where urgent consignments are not available for collection until a late hour, special arrangements are made whereby it can be delivered to us for dispatch by the "Dawn Express."

Every weekday just before dawn, the Multi-engined Air Freighter leaves Croydon Aerodrome for Paris where it arrives one and a half hours later, where all customs facilities are attended to, and in less than two hours after leaving Croydon, goods are delivered to any address in Paris.

Where consignments are sent to destinations South of Paris, these are transferred to Services leaving Le Bourget for Lyons and the Riviera, where parcels will be delivered a few hours later.

Through rates are quoted on application.

RATES

LONDON—PARIS

The Rates quoted hereunder are from Domicile to Domicile, but do not include unbonding, for which an extra charge of 6d. (sixpence) per parcel is charged.

Insurance will be arranged by the Company where especially required.

COLLECTION AND DELIVERY

Goods are collected from any address within the City and West End of London, or they can be handed in to Messrs. Crowe & Co., 37 Upper Thames Street, London, E.C.4. Notification for collection should be made by telephone not later than 4 p.m. to Central 5050 (Ex. 13). After this time particulars of consignment should be telephoned to Croydon 5122.

57 The inside pages of an Air Dispatch publicity leaflet

only newspaper to reach Parisian breakfast tables that morning.

Carrying newspapers was not profitable, and only Imperial Airways received any subsidy. Quite a few of our competitors went out of business. We always knew when they were on their way out, because they would leave sad little notes outside their office, saying 'No milk today please'.

Despite difficult flying conditions, Air Dispatch had a fine accident-free record for three years. I don't think we missed more than one service a year during the time we had the newspaper contract. We bought two more Dragons and started an ambulance service. This was most successful, generally fully booked. We then had a crew of five pilots and five wireless operators, all of whom took instruction in first aid.

As I was Managing Director of Air Dispatch the Commodore of the aerodrome requested me to report to the control tower whenever the weather was foggy because I was expected to give instructions as to where I wished my pilots to land. An official would then transmit my instructions over the wireless. It was a very worrying task for me when there was widespread fog. Scarcely a month passed during the winter months without my being called up in the middle of the night to come to the control tower.

About 1937 a patch of accidents struck. Gloom descended on Croydon. First it was the turn of KLM, then Air France. Then us.

One foggy morning about 6.30 a.m., the telephone woke me up. It was an officer in the Croydon control tower. Our pilot had taken off at 3.30 a.m. but had not reached Paris, and the radio operator had sent a message that they were flying blind. I dressed and hurried to the control tower.

It appeared from the bearing the pilot gave that he was right off course and flying at only 1,000 feet. The hills around Croydon are quite high, and I became very anxious when no further message was received. By eight o'clock I feared the worst and a search party was organised. I set off in a hired aircraft, scouring the country between Croydon and the Channel; no trace of the missing aircraft could be found. We were all searching by that time; several other aircraft operators were helping. By nightfall there was still no news of the Dawn Express.

Seventeen hours passed before a message came from the police at Westerham. Someone had telephoned to say they had heard an explosion like a clap of thunder near Titsey Hill. We made our way there. The plane had been found: it was a total loss and the wreckage was spread all round. The crew had been killed instantly. Newspapers were blowing about all over the road up the hill. The machine had hit the branches of the trees at the very top of the hill.

There was at least a more fortunate outcome of another incident. A few weeks later another of our planes was struck by lightning, but that time the crew escaped unhurt.

Apart from the human tragedy, the crash of the Dawn Express dealt a heavy blow to Air Dispatch. I could see the moment coming when we, too would have to put out a notice: 'No milk today.' Salvation came in a mysterious fashion.

Late one evening a man arrived at the aerodrome and asked to see me. He found me just as I was going home in the car. It was late, and I was tired: the worry of the newspaper service was beginning to tell. Wearily I wound down the window; he said 'I want to buy your aeroplanes.'

I asked: 'Which ones?' 'All of them,' he replied. I told him not to be silly, I was running an airline. But he persisted: 'I'll pay you three times their value.' I felt the matter was at least worthy of my interest. The conversation continued: 'Will ambulance machines do? If so they're yours.'

He went into the hangar and inspected one of the Dragons. Then he said, 'Your price please'. 'Ten thousand pounds for the two of them', I said casually, although I was quaking, because it certainly was about three times their value.

'It's a deal; the money will be given to you at dawn tomorrow, provided the machines are ready on the tarmac with two pilots.' 'Where are they going,' I asked. 'To France' was his reply. Telling him he must find his own pilots, I left for home.

At dawn the following morning I was at the aerodrome. The two Dragons were already lined up outside the hangar. Within a few minutes the mystery man arrived carrying a black bag. He pulled out a small packet from it and produced ten bank notes. My chief pilot, there to see that no confidence trick was likely, examined them and said, 'They're £1,000 notes.' I had never heard of a £1,000 note, let alone seen one. I was about to take them when the man said, 'Wait, they're not yours yet, have the engines started up first, please.'

Being suspicious, I drove across the aerodrome to the Custom Control office. An officer told me the stranger had clearance papers. I drove back and asked my chief pilot to start the engines up. The man now handed me the notes and I counted them three times. Then for the first time, and I felt sure for the last time, I had ten £1,000 notes in my handbag. I waited for a while. Then two pilots arrived in a car. I knew one of them and asked him: 'Where are the planes going?' He said, 'First to

France, then to Spain. They're needed as ambulance machines for the Civil War.'

As soon as the machines left, I drove to my local bank in Whaddon, a few miles from Croydon. When the manager saw me at the counter counting the notes, he closed the bank doors. He then counted them himself, and said there were only nine. 'That's impossible,' I cried, 'I've counted them about ten times; I've nearly worn them out!' He counted them again. Ten, this time; two had been sticking together! He told me that until the Bank of England had examined them he would not know whether they were genuine. The thought of forgery had never struck me. I spent a sleepless night – but next morning the Bank of England gave the notes the green light.

Twenty-four hours earlier we were almost down to our last propeller: now the bank manager was asking if I wanted to open a deposit account.

With the money we bought two De Havilland Rapide twin-engined eight-seaters, and an Avro 642 built by Saunders Roe, which carried sixteen passengers. Using the Avro, we started a passenger service to Paris. I gave instructions for it to be painted blue, and called the service the 'Blue Plane'. (This was about the time when the Blue Train to the South of France was so popular). We became Britain's fastest airline on the route.

There were no air hostesses in 1937. The idea for them struck me when I was thinking about stewards for the Blue Plane. I decided to advertise and see if any girls were interested. No sooner had the advertisement appeared than the phone began to ring. Never were there so many letters; the enthusiasm was enormous. Many had to be disappointed, for the idea of a hostess in an aeroplane was something new, and no one else was offering jobs.

A very attractive blonde was the first to call at our control office at Croydon, and I engaged her on the spot. Her name was Daphne Vickers. I wondered if she would feel nervous, but she settled down to the job at once, and the passengers took to the idea of an air hostess. Daphne had great charm, and gave confidence to both male and female passengers, which was especially valuable to those making their first-ever flight.

We provided lunch and champagne, and although I was never very anxious to fly unless I was the pilot, on the second day of launching the service I decided to fly in the Blue Plane to Paris.

Just as we reached the English Channel I noticed notes were being exchanged between the pilot and the wireless operator. 'What is wrong,' I worried. Then I saw the wireless operator make a thumbs down gesture, and the pilot shrugged his shoulders. Whether Daphne or the passengers noticed all this I don't know, but I began to think the end of the journey was near at hand. It was with a sigh of relief that I saw Le Bourget aerodrome in the distance.

After landing, I decided to have a word with the pilot in case there was something wrong with the engines. He explained that the conversation with the wireless operator was of a purely personal character; after further questioning I extracted from him the information that the matter under discussion was to do with an appointment with a girl friend in Paris. Returning to Croydon, I made arrangements for a door to be fixed between the pilot's cockpit, and the passenger lounge.

One day one of our competitors in the air freight business dropped a consignment of gold bars (worth half a million pounds) through the floorboards of their Dragon aircraft. The boxes of gold fell into someone's back garden, and were not noticed for two days. What a commotion! Underwriters at Lloyds were kept in suspense, and I thought that was the time for me to call upon the chief underwriter. I told him that our big Avro had a metal floor; would he advise the bullion merchants Samuel Montague that their gold would be safer in our plane? I hoped I might get the contract for Air Dispatch, and the rate paid for carrying bullion was five times the ordinary rate for freight.

Within a week we received a contract.

We were allowed to be armed when carrying bullion, so I promptly bought and licensed two ·45 Colts. The revolvers did not frighten me after my experience in Los Angeles when I had the ash shot from my cigarette at the police headquarters. The young traffic clerk would accompany me in my AC coupé to London, and the bullion merchants would put half a dozen boxes of bars in the dicky of the car. (The value was generally around half a million pounds.) I am sure if we tried to do this today we would be knocked on the head within a few minutes.

By this time we had a fleet of three Dragons, and two De Havilland Rapides, also twin engined eight-seater planes. Soon we started another service: the 'Inner Circle Airline'.

We ran it around London – a sort of Tube of the air, linking up the various airports: Heston, Hanworth, Gatwick and others. We arranged for passengers to go aboard and buy their tickets from the pilot, as if on a bus. It was a great success.

Our first passengers were two school children. Their mother had moved to Croydon but wished the children to continue their schooling in Hounslow on the other side of London. It was a two-hour journey to Hounslow by car, but only five minutes by air. We gave the children a season ticket, £1 2s. 6d. weekly. It must have been the first season ticket of the air.

The idea caused great excitement. People started writing to the children and sending them presents; they even had letters from as far away as America. If it hadn't been for the War I feel sure that this 'Tube of the Air' would have grown into a very important service because it was so very useful for getting from one side of London to the other.

During these years, Croydon was a very happy place to operate from. It was the main terminal at the time, and the famous aerodrome hotel was most popular with pilots and passengers. There were a number of independent operators at Croydon apart from the national line then known as Imperial Airways.

Surrey Flying Services offered ten-shilling flights over London, and also ran a charter company, Olley Air Services; this was run by Captain Olley, a most experienced pilot who had recently retired from Imperial Airways. Then there was Rollason Air Services, managed and owned by Captain Rollason; he could put a Dragon down more or less on a tennis lawn, and his firm were experts in aircraft maintenance.

It was about October 1937 that we obtained a Government contract for Army co-operation flying. This meant flying in the searchlights for the Territorial Army, who were practising with their guns, sound-locators and searchlights. The Air Force was too busy to continue such work, and it was contracted to us to supply aircraft for the job.

Germany was arming at a frightening speed, so I decided to curtail the airline activities, buy more aircraft, and concentrate on Government work. (This proved to be just as well; the Munich Crisis was near.) Within three months we had bought five more Rapides and engaged five more pilots and wireless operators.

In Army co-operation flying we used to fly at 12,000 feet over London, while the searchlights tried to pick us up in their beams. Up and down the Edgware Road was one of our allotted courses: it may sound funny, but we were actually overhead that route.

There was a Major attached to the searchlight brigade – I can't remember his name – who used to complain that we were never over the course and grumbled a great deal. We were there all right, but the lights couldn't reach us at 12,000 feet. (Perhaps it was just as well we didn't go to war during the Munich Crisis; it was a long time before the searchlights were powerful enough to reach us.) The Major continued to grumble, despite our explanation. We dreaded the thought of upsetting him with anything at all, so much so that one night, being short of a pilot, I asked a young Japanese pilot who used to borrow my little aircraft sometimes – I'd known him since he was at school – if he would fly the course that night as a favour. What a row that caused! I was sent for by the War Office. What did I mean by letting a Japanese fly over London? they wanted to know. When I arrived there were four staff officers, including a Brigadier, sitting round a table. I tried to explain that it had happened because of The Major. I mentioned The Major at least three times.

The Brigadier said he was puzzled: 'What is all this talk

about "The Major"? Who is he? Is this his *nom de plume*?'

'Oh no!' I said. '*That's* not his *nom de plume*; his *nom de plume's* "The *Barmy* Major".'

I thought I noticed a smile pass over the face of the Brigadier.

'Well . . . ', he said at length, 'We have listened to her story, have heard senior officers called 'Barmy', and have had to put up with a Japanese flying in our searchlights.' Turning from his colleagues to me, he admonished: 'You are dismissed madam, we will give you the verdict in due course.'

The next day I rang the Director of Contracts at the Air Ministry.

'You are forgiven,' he said, 'but in future no foreigners are to fly on Army co-operation work. You will receive a new contract tomorrow, and in it this will be stated clearly.'

The Major, however, continued to grumble, and still insisted we were not over the course; he even refused to sign the bills at the end of the month. In desperation we suggested he should come up one night and see for himself. Our Chief Pilot took him up over twelve thousand feet; he was frozen.

'Get me down,' he said. 'I never dreamt we were so bad.' (In fact he said something much worse than that!) The searchlights beamed all over the sky – but at least three thousand feet below their targets.

'What about the bills, Sir?' our pilot suggested.

'Okay. Send them in again.'

We had no further trouble. After that night I paid many visits to the various searchlight positions.

By 1938 we had twenty-three aeroplanes, nineteen of which were twin-engined, eight-seater airliners: Dragons and Rapides. All of these were working on Army co-operation flying.

The fact that Army co-operation took place at night meant that I was usually free in the daytime. I had maintained my early interest in ponies, and I often thought of the day when I would get a show-jumper. My ambition was to take part in the International Horse Show at Olympia. About 1937, I bought a little pony and practised over some jumps in a field by my house in Chipstead, whenever I had the time to spare.

I knew the three Carter brothers, who were all International riders; one day, on a visit to London, I met them . . .

58 The cover of a publicity leaflet

Fourteen

International Horse Show

IN THE COURSE of conversation, Len Carter, the youngest of the brothers, asked me if I would like to buy a 'wonderful grey'.

'Can he jump?' I asked.

'He could jump a traction engine,' was the reply. 'If you'd like to come down to our stables in Barnes, we'll show you what he can do.'

Within half an hour I reached the stables. Soon Len led out a sultry-eyed grey, and mounting, took him over a jump (it must have been at least six feet five) consisting of two gates with a terrific spread, and an iron bar in the middle. I couldn't imagine any horse getting over a jump like that, but he cleared it by about a foot.

Then Len said to me : 'Up you go; you go over.' 'No fear,' I said, 'Not over that.'

It was never any good to argue with Len, and before I knew where I was he gave me a leg up, and the next thing I was over that mighty jump. 'What a wonderful horse,' I thought.

'His name is Grand Manner,' said Len.

Then Bob Carter came across from the stables and told me that the horse was entered for the International Horse Show at Olympia and that he hoped to win the Daily Mail Gold Cup.

'You can ride him if you like instead of Len; although if you win he will be worth several thousand pounds, and then we shall probably sell him to the Italians.'

I had a feeling that horse could win anything, so I asked how much it would cost to buy him.

'Two hundred pounds,' said Bob, and then he added: 'You two ought to get on together; you are both always full out.'

The thought that if I won the Cup I might have to let the horse go to Italy was more than I could bear, so I said: 'I'll have him. When do I start to practise?' (I wanted to take Grand Manner over that terrific jump once more.)

'Better not practise on this horse,' said Bob, as he started to lead him away towards the stables. 'You'll see him the day after tomorrow at Olympia, and not before. He needs no practice; nothing will stop him; he'll jump anything,' Bob said, and then added in an undertone: 'So long as you can get him over the first jump.'

On Friday night I arrived at Olympia. My number was 72, so I had some hours to wait before my turn to jump.

In the collecting ring, just outside the main ring, beautifully groomed horses were being slowly ridden around. I immediately looked for the Carter brothers, but I couldn't find them at first. So I searched the stables, and there at the end of the block was Grand Manner. He looked magnificent: his tail had been beautifully brushed and his long mane made him look to me like some of the pictures of a Roman scene. I gave him a lump of sugar and patted him on the neck: he seemed to like me. Presently Len Carter came up and tied the '72' round my waist. It looked as though it would be midnight before I entered the ring. It was then only nine o'clock, and the time passed slowly. I had already looked at the jumps – they were set out in a figure of eight – and tried to memorize them. After a time I went up into the stalls where my son Tony was waiting for me. By eleven o'clock there had been nothing better than eight faults.

At 11.15 I was back at the stables. Bob Carter said: 'Up you go'. Then he led us to the collecting ring. 'Now, slowly does it,' he explained. 'Walk him round for another five minutes, then walk again until your turn comes. I will lead you in.'

I began to feel like one of the early Christians before they were thrown to the lions in the arena. Grand Manner was a very temperamental horse ('hot' we called it) and he liked to be led into the ring or he was liable to become too excited.

At last my turn came. As Bob led us into the arena I heard someone say, 'This one ain't going to be much good.'

59 At the Royal International Horse Show, Olympia
Col. Llewellyn was first, myself second

The starter gave the word 'Go'. Grand Manner tried to turn and dash back through the great doors, but by some wonderful stroke of luck I managed to turn him back towards the first jump. I remembered Bob's warning about it.

I was in a most difficult position, and I had to take the jump sideways; I just managed it, and the next jump down by the hydrangeas. (There were always lovely flowers at the end of the arena at Olympia: more appropriate to a funeral, I thought, as I tried to steady Grand Manner.) Then I was off again over the single pole (always a difficult jump), to the gate.

By now I was going full gallop. Feeling sure he knew more about it than I did, I let him go. I was not sure whether we were going the right way as I tried to remember the figure of eight. Then we reached the wall, which I was told afterwards Grand Manner cleared by about a foot. Then over the open ditch; the stile; then the double oxer, which nobody had cleared during

60 In action at Lingfield

the evening. At full gallop Grand Manner romped down the finishing straight, and the great doors opened. The Carters were waiting, looking very pleased.

'Have I a clear round?' I asked. 'Not quite, half a fault', was the reply. (In those days, slats were placed on top of all the jumps; if you knocked one off, it cost half a fault.) I was happy; I hadn't expected to find my way round that course.

I went up to the starter who was sitting on a high ladder and said: 'Excuse me, but is there a prize for fastest time?' He looked down at me and said, 'If there was I'd give it to you.'

I went up and sat next to my son Tony who had been watching. He was encouraging: 'Mother, you may be all right; there are only five more to come into the ring. You'll probably win the Daily Mail Gold Cup.'

But the next horse to come in was a lovely bay, Silver Mint, and it was ridden by Colonel Llewellyn. Over the jumps he went, in grand style until he came to the double oxer. His horse touched it; it shook. For a moment it looked as though it would fall, but it didn't: he had a clear round. That was the night I missed the Daily Mail Gold Cup.

Following on my near success, I decided to have some advanced lessons in jumping, so I went to Faudell Phillips' school in Hertfordshire. They made me start at the beginning, although I kept telling Major Phillips that I had nearly won at Olympia; he only replied, 'That was the horse, not you'. Right up to the outbreak of war I continued to practise, and to enter various jumping competitions.

I was rewarded in the end, for in 1939 I was first in the Open Jumping class at the Royal Horse Show at Windsor – on the sultry-eyed grey!

Fifteen
Sealed Orders

AIR DISPATCH continued to flourish at this time, and soon after the Munich Crisis, an official from the Air Ministry called at my office in Croydon. He asked whether my company would be prepared to sign a dormant contract, one which would become operative only in the event of a national emergency, when our entire fleet of twenty-three aircraft would be subject to any order from the Air Ministry.

As 'Air Dispatch' was more or less 'me', I agreed to sign. Before the official left, he told me I would receive sealed orders, to be opened only if a dispatch with a special code word was delivered. He went on to say that there would be three messages in the event of an emergency. The first would be 'Get ready to stand by'. On receiving this, all pilots and wireless operators were to be told to report to the aerodrome every two hours. On receipt of the second dispatch, 'Stand by', the complete fleet were to be lined up on the tarmac, and engines started up every hour.

If and when the third dispatch arrived, with the code word 'Lascelle', the crews were to remain in the aircraft and await a signal from the control tower ordering them to take off. Only then I was to open the sealed orders, which contained details of the secret bases to which the pilots were to go.

Within a few days I signed the contract, and the sealed orders were delivered and put in the safe.

Life went on as usual for about nine months and we carried on with the army co-operation flying. Then on the morning of 31 August 1939, the first message was delivered by a dispatch-rider from the war office. 'Get ready to stand by.' All pilots and wireless operators who were operating in the Midlands and

Wales were recalled to Croydon. The next day the second message arrived: 'Stand by.' The fleet was at once lined up on the tarmac and engines started up every hour. Lorries were loaded with spares. The aerodrome was blacked out and great bulldozers were digging trenches round the aerodrome hotel, tearing up the geraniums. Everyone was tense and resigned for the worst.

The suspense was broken on the evening of 1 September. I had just arrived home and was putting the key in the lock of the front door when I heard the telephone ringing. It was the young traffic clerk. He said he had just received a special message delivered by a dispatch rider from the War Office. He started to spell it out slowly: 'L . . . A . . . S . . . C . . . ' 'Stop,' I cried, 'I will come down to the aerodrome immediately.'

I reached my office and opened the sealed orders. It was war. Within an hour ten of our planes left for RAF bases, and the remainder for Cardiff, which was to be our wartime base.

For the next eight months we operated a ferry service to France, carrying high-ranking RAF personnel; and we carried supplies (many of which were later to be abandoned at Dunkirk).

The phoney war was on, but that was soon to end. About the middle of May, Captain Scott (one of our senior pilots) returned from France to the Cardiff base. 'France has fallen', he said. 'The roads are full of nuns winding up their puttees.' 'What *do* you mean?' we asked, 'German soldiers, disguised,' he said, 'blowing up the bridges.'

The phoney war was over. Within two weeks, all our aircraft were requisitioned and most of our key personnel called up. We were left with one week in which to secure some kind of Air Ministry contract, or lose all our key personnel. Trunk calls were put through to almost every aircraft factory of any importance in the country, but without result. At last, a call to Helliwells of Walsall was successful. Forty wings were available for repair – but alas, no transport. It was impossible at that time to obtain transport anywhere, but there was still my horse box. Within twelve hours it was converted to carry eight wings,

61 Part of the fleet of De Haviland Rapides

and in a few days we were collecting these from Helliwells. The Company's troubles were not over yet, however.

It turned out that permission was necessary from the Air Ministry, if one was to work on aircraft, or parts of aircraft, belonging to the RAF; to get this permission was very difficult.

I hurried up to London to see Lord Beaverbrook at the Ministry of Aircraft Production. Now, it was practically impossible to get an appointment with him; everything had first to be put in writing. This would mean precious days lost, and only five days were left to save the organisation and to inform the Air Ministry that the Company was on work of national importance and entitled to keep their key men.

Reaching London I found it was as I expected: it was impossible to see Lord Beaverbrook. I decided to wait outside the office in the hope of obtaining an interview with Mr Freeman, his right hand man. After many patient hours of waiting Mr Freeman emerged and gruffly asked what the vitally urgent business was about. More anxious moments! I tried to convince him that the country could not possibly win the War without Air Dispatch. His remark at the end of the interview was that if the enthusiasm and energy shown in trying to get an interview with him could be put into the repair of the wings, then there was not much doubt that Air Dispatch would make a success of the venture . . .

The gloom of the last few days at Cardiff lifted: busy hands began to unload the first consignment of wings, and so from this small beginning a new organisation came into being.

The months rolled by. Cardiff received its first air raid. Hundreds of wings began arriving at the aerodrome. They no longer came by horse box any more; transport was now supplied by MAP. Soon crashed machines arrived as well. We were told that for every three aircraft broken, one could be repaired – and it had to be if we were to win the War. An eighty-hour week was started at our Cardiff factory, which was already employing over four hundred people.

One night on my return from Cardiff, just as I approached the gates of the drive to my house at Westonbirt, I was challenged. I had nearly run into a huge tree trunk stetched across the road in the blackout. 'Stop!' An old-fashioned rifle was pushed through my car window.

'What *do* you think you are doing, Cobb?' I asked: it was my groom – in the Home Guard now – being over-enthusiastic. As I told my friends afterwards, he reminded me of a cartoon I'd seen of a sentry, standing with a smoking rifle in his hands and shouting, 'Who went there?'

I still had some things from previous, more normal years: I had moved my show-jumpers to my country home in Gloucestershire. They grazed peacefully there. But one day a man from the Air Ministry called at my house. 'Your land will make a good satellite aerodrome,' he informed me. Amongst many other questions, I asked, 'What about the horses? Where will they graze?'

'Forget them. You'll be eating them soon,' had been his miserable reply. Eat Grand Manner? Never! I put him to work on a farm cart together with the others and they grazed in a small paddock near the house.

Soon we were surrounded by bombers. Stirlings they were, all hidden in a large wood which bordered the estate, and guarded by Alsatian dogs. As it happened they were never used but it was a consolation to know they were there if needed. The Battle of Britain had been fought and won.

Broken aircraft still poured in by lorry to Cardiff, and everyone was working long hours, weekdays and weekends. The spirit of the people was wonderful. We had to carry on while events happend like that of 10 May 1941 which was afterwards described as 'The Battle of the Full Moon'. Bombs rained down from the sky. Fires blazed all over London. Cardiff was hit again. Bristol was in flames. The monotonous drone of the Nazi planes disturbed the quiet of the night. In the morning a pall of smoke over the towns hid the ruins beneath. Britain was burning. Our work continued apace as the months came and went. The war dragged on: the people hoped.

I remember one morning in 1944, when thousands of aeroplanes appeared overhead, towing gliders. The horses panicked, tearing round the field. Only the year before two thousand-pounders had dropped in the garden – meant for our satellite landing ground. No wonder the horses were frightened!

Then D-Day arrived. The bomb was soon to drop on Hiroshima. Nevertheless for the next eight months Air Dispatch continued to increase its output. A further contract was secured, for the repair of Harvard aircraft, and another for the production of pontoons for use in Japan. Then the bomb had dropped on Hiroshima. The war was over.

The various repair organisations now began to curtail their output; thoughts were turned towards peace and the future. We received instructions from MAP to finish the Harvards and Pontoons. There was to be no further contract. The work could easily be completed in six months. For the second time, gloom descended on Air Dispatch. The competition of nationalised companies prevented Air Dispatch from succeeding at its previous peacetime occupation of running international air services. Air Dispatch made a spirited fight on behalf of the private airline operators, supported by numerous MPs, to try to get sufficient licensing of routes for private operators.

Success was just in sight when the Government fell. A new Government was elected and the five pioneer airline operators, one of the largest being Air Dispatch, were cast aside.

The nationalised airlines needed skilled personnel, and the key men of Air Dispatch were again about to leave as they had done at the start of the war, seeing no future for the Company. Air Dispatch had the choice of shutting its doors or launching out on some new type of business.

I approached the Regional Controller of the Ministry of Supply, Cardiff. He was most anxious that Air Dispatch should continue its activities, and promised me that if we would keep the organisation going he would recommend our Company for suitable contracts. There is no doubt that meeting Mr Smith and agreeing to carry on created a very favourable impression with the Ministry of Supply. Our Company as a whole was in excellent shape (and the Air Ministry had commented that the accounts department was easily the best of the forty repair organisations).

We were particularly pleased to receive a letter from Air Vice Marshall Fraser, congratulating us on the work we had carried out for the RAF.

Just before the last Harvard was completed, Tony, who had now left the Army, joined the Company again. It was not long before he got things moving. We were at this time employing about seven hundred people, and it was vital to keep them employed. He approached a firm in Lancashire who were building motor bus bodies, and suggested they give us any overflow work. They were pleased to do this as they had a contract with the Cardiff Corporation to build the bodies for their new trolley buses, when the trams were being scrapped. Within a year the first trolley bus was produced – and duly blessed by the Lord Mayor of Cardiff outside Cardiff Town Hall. We ended up building all the trolley bus bodies for Cardiff and other bus bodies for Corporations all over England.

Then for the third time gloom descended upon Air Dispatch. There was an aluminium shortage! We could not get enough to keep twenty buses on the production line. We gradually had to cut down, and had to lose most of our key men. We started to repair other buses in the hope of keeping going, but we were soon working on only five buses, and were running at a loss.

The factory had to close, the Company of Air Dispatch was no longer.

Epilogue

NO LONGER having the time-consuming business of running Air Dispatch, I began to search for more records to tackle. I was very keen to take up motor racing again. But my family and friends felt I should give up these dangerous pursuits, and advised me to go in for something solid and safe: bricks and mortar, they suggested.

I decided to take this advice. I had soon signed a contract for a lease on two large houses in Bryanston Square. Most of the houses had been bombed, and the Square looked desolate, but I formed a building company, and began to convert the damaged houses into flats.

Within seven days of this new venture's start, I was in the casualty ward of the Middlesex hospital. A workman had dropped his sledge hammer from the first floor, and it had landed on my foot. I had barely recovered from this, when I stepped on a floorboard left the wrong way up with a large nail projecting. The nail went right through my foot, and within ten minutes, I was back in the Middlesex.

I had taken many risks; I had been involved in three aircraft crashes; I had never before received emergency treatment. I decided that it was downright dangerous for me to undertake any job which others might consider safe.

Index

The Hon. Mrs Victor Bruce (Mary Bruce) is abbreviated here as MB